High-Impact
African-American Churches

George Barna and Bishop Harry Jackson, Jr., have ably brought together their considerable natural and spiritual gifts to produce this significant resource book *High-Impact African-American Churches*. They rightly see that no people group can survive an attack of the magnitude of what black Americans have experience unless the people group gets itself right with God.

This book will give people an opportunity to look at America's sins against its brothers and sisters and will also cause people to break into rejoicing as they read what God has done for the least of these among us. I believe that the information in this book will help build bridges between the races. Racism in America is the taunting Goliath that disproves all the Church's talk of love. Reconciliation through Christ is the David that will bring it down.

Hold on! We are about to become that unified Church Jesus prayed for. Together, we can win the world for Christ. *High-Impact African-American Churches* is a sign that it can be done.

Bishop Wellington Boone

PASTOR, THE FATHER'S HOUSE
NORCROSS, GEORGIA

While the focus of this work is on African-American churches, *High-Impact African-American Churches* is a must-read for pastors of all backgrounds and all races. The innovative ideas will help high-impact leaders develop great churches across the nation. Harry Jackson and George Barna set a good direction for other churches to consider.

Bob Buford

AUTHOR, *HALFTIME: MOVING FROM SUCCESS TO SIGNIFICANCE*
FOUNDING CHAIRMAN, LEADERSHIP NETWORK

High-Impact African-American Churches is a rich mine of
practical and spiritual images that will empower and
inspire your local church to pursue undeniable greatness for
God! Thank God for George and Harry!

KIRBYJON H. CALDWELL

COAUTHOR, *ENTREPRENEURIAL FAITH*
PASTOR, WINDSOR VILLAGE UNITED METHODIST CHURCH
HOUSTON, TEXAS

The African-American church is not only a central institution of the
African-American community, but it also has important lessons to
share with the broader Christian Church. George Barna, a
market pollster with an international reputation, and Bishop
Harry Jackson, a church leader with a rich experience in the
urban black community, make a dynamic duo. Each contributes to
the other in providing a study that is both fascinating and
comprehensive. Here are valuable lessons for all to ponder, especially
for churches engaged in urban ministry. Urban contexts represent
the cultural powerhouses of American society, in which the African-
American churches are still influential and respected.

DR. EDDIE GIBBS

PROFESSOR OF CHURCH GROWTH, FULLER THEOLOGICAL SEMINARY

In this book, George Barna and Bishop Harry Jackson present candid
and compelling insights describing God's work among African-
American churches. The empirical research dismantles the stereotypes
about the inferiority of the African-American church and
validates the truth of Scripture that God does not discriminate
in the distribution of gifts to His Church.

DR. LARRY A. MERCER

SENIOR VICE PRESIDENT, MEDIA AND CHURCH MINISTRIES
THE MOODY BIBLE INSTITUTE

Bishop Harry Jackson, an experienced African-American pastor, and George Barna, a skilled Caucasian-American researcher, have combined to write a landmark study of the African-American church. *High-Impact African-American Churches* highlights the holistic integration of doctrine and life with a focus on the best practices of quality, high-impact churches. African-Americans can learn how to do church more effectively; Caucasian-Americans can learn how to combine faith and works more biblically.

JOHN PERKINS

FOUNDER, JOHN M. PERKINS FOUNDATION FOR
RECONCILIATION AND DEVELOPMENT

For years, most Christian leaders have admired the amazing and profound religious and social impact of black churches in our cities. Now my friends, George Barna and Harry Jackson have focused a brilliant floodlight on African-American churches, allowing us to see clearly how they have gone about doing it. *High-Impact African-American Churches* is important reading!

C. PETER WAGNER

AUTHOR, *CHURCHQUAKE!* AND *OUT OF AFRICA*
CHANCELLOR, WAGNER LEADERSHIP INSTITUTE

HIGH IMPACT

AFRICAN-AMERICAN

CHURCHES

GEORGE BARNA

HARRY R. JACKSON, JR.

Regal

From Gospel Light
Ventura, California, U.S.A.

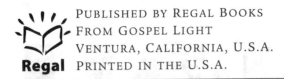

PUBLISHED BY REGAL BOOKS
FROM GOSPEL LIGHT
VENTURA, CALIFORNIA, U.S.A.
Regal PRINTED IN THE U.S.A.

Regal Books is a ministry of Gospel Light, a Christian publisher dedicated to serving the local church. We believe God's vision for Gospel Light is to provide church leaders with biblical, user-friendly materials that will help them evangelize, disciple and minister to children, youth and families.

It is our prayer that this Regal book will help you discover biblical truth for your own life and help you meet the needs of others. May God richly bless you.

For a free catalog of resources from Regal Books/Gospel Light, please call your Christian supplier or contact us at 1-800-4-GOSPEL *or* www.regalbooks.com.

All information included in the church profiles was gathered through personal interviews with and contributions from the individual churches.

Cover design by David Griffing
Interior design by Stephen Hahn
Edited by Mia Kaely

Library of Congress Cataloging-in-Publication Data

Barna, George.
  High-impact African-American churches / George Barna and Harry Jackson.
    p. cm.
  Includes bibliographical references.
  ISBN 0-8307-3898-3 (hardcover), ISBN 0-8307-3265-9 (trade paper)
  1. African American churches. 2. Leadership—Religious aspects—Christianity. I. Jackson, Harry R. II. Title.
  BR563.N4B375 2004
  253'.089'96073—dc22   2004008429

1 2 3 4 5 6 7 8 9 10 11 12 13 14 15 16 / 14 13 12 11 10 09 08 07 06 05

Rights for publishing this book in other languages are contracted by Gospel Light Worldwide, the international nonprofit ministry of Gospel Light. Gospel Light Worldwide also provides publishing and technical assistance to international publishers dedicated to producing Sunday School and Vacation Bible School curricula and books in the languages of the world. For additional information, visit www.gospellightworldwide.org; write to Gospel Light Worldwide, P.O. Box 3875, Ventura, CA 93006; or send an e-mail to info@gospellightworldwide.org.

DEDICATION

This book is respectfully dedicated to people who have made a unique contribution to the African-American church during the last 100 years. The names listed here represent just a sampling of thousands of black leaders who have tirelessly served both the Lord and their community. The following names are listed in alphabetical order instead of rank or significance.

E. K. Bailey (1946-2003) founded Concord Missionary Baptist Church, a model African-American megachurch from which he trained thousands of leaders in effective sermon preparation, church growth and leadership principles. Dr. Bailey was catalytic in creating many black megachurches.

Wellington Boone is one of the first African-Americans to break through into a national multiracial ministry arena. Bishop Boone's messages have emphasized racial reconciliation, holiness and family development.

Juanita Bynum is best known for her fiery messages and straightforward delivery of biblical truths. Her honest depiction of lifestyle pressures and temptations of the average African-American woman has made her one of the most celebrated black preachers of the twenty-first century. Her classic book *No More Sheets* has challenged African-American women to lead a consecrated life for God.

Floyd Flake, senior pastor of Allen AME Church in Queens, New York, has been a change agent within the New York community and the world. Locally, Allen Temple's $24 million operation is a paradigm of church and nonprofit efficiency. Nationally, Dr. Flake has also served as a United States Congressman and president of Wilberforce University.

E. V. Hill (1934-2003) was best known as a bridge builder in the Body of Christ. Loved by millions, he was an ambassador for the black church to the nations. His bold sermons were often heard not only in conferences but also in frequent appearances on television and radio.

T. D. Jakes is often referred to as a "shepherd to the shattered" because he has preached his messages to millions of hurting women and men around the globe. As the senior pastor of the 24,000-member church The Potter's House in Dallas, Texas, Bishop Jakes has created a powerful local base for his groundbreaking international ministry. In 1999, the *New York Times* named him "one of the top five evangelists" and *Time* magazine named him "America's Best Preacher" in 2001.

Martin Luther King, Jr. (1929-1968) was *Time* magazine's Man of the Year in 1963 and the recipient of the Nobel Peace Prize in 1964. Along with Abraham Lincoln, Dr. King stands as the most visible champion of civil rights in American history. His life and ministry not only brought dignity to the individual black person in the nation, but they also brought great dignity to the role of African-American ministry and ministers. This book could have been dedicated to him alone.

Eddie Long is the senior pastor of New Birth Missionary Baptist Church in Lithonia, Georgia, which has grown from 300 members in 1987 to 25,000 members today. At one time his church was arguably the largest church in North America. Bishop Long has inspired thousands of African-American leaders to pursue the kingdom of God and to impact their regions for Christ.

Vashti Mackenzie pastored Payne Memorial AME Church in Baltimore, Maryland, where she decided to take back the neighborhood streets from drugs and poverty. Rev. Mackenzie so excelled in urban leadership that she gained the distinction of becoming the first female bishop of the 213-year-old AME Church.

C. H. Mason (1866-1961) was the founder of the Church of God in Christ (COGIC). Bishop Mason's prayer life, personal holiness and practical wisdom are legendary among African-American church leaders. Today the COGIC claims more than 8 million members.

Paul Morton is the senior pastor of the 20,000-member Greater St. Stephens Full Gospel Baptist Church and founder of the Full Gospel Baptist Church denomination. Under Bishop Morton's leadership, the Full Gospel Baptist Church's combined membership has reached nearly 1 million people.

G. E. Patterson is senior pastor of Temple of Deliverance Church of God in Christ in Memphis, Tennessee. The church has had a direct impact on unemployment, education, health and family life within the city. Nationally, Rev. Patterson has worked hard to maintain the legacy of C. H. Mason by serving as the presiding bishop of the Church of God in Christ. In addition, Bishop Patterson was a contributing writer for the *Spirit Filled Life Bible (KJV)* and hosts an international television ministry.

Betty Peebles is the apostle and senior pastor of Jericho City of Praise, a congregation that occupies the 200,000-square-foot complex adjacent to the Washington Redskins' FedEx stadium. Rev. Peebles has been an example for Christian women by maintaining a strong family life while pastoring the largest church in the nation under female leadership.

John Perkins was the first to develop the concept of the Christian Community Development Association (CCDA), where churches could receive funds from businesses and government in order to revitalize the communities in which they served. This relentless pioneer has also advanced the concept of racial reconciliation throughout the world.

William Seymour (1870-1922) became the catalyst of the Pentecostal Movement in the twentieth century after his Azusa Street stable in Los Angeles became an international center of revival. People from around the world came to the Azusa Street Mission to become part of the interracial services. As a result, missionaries were sent to several continents. Seymour's work had a seminal effect on both the Church of God in Christ (black) and its offshoot, The Assemblies of God (white).

Tom Skinner (1942-1994) formed the Harlem Evangelistic Association, which eventually expanded to national and international locations. In the 1970s, Skinner was dubbed a "black Billy Graham" in evangelical circles. In addition to his crusade ministry, Tom Skinner Associates established campus outreaches, conducted motivational seminars, created publications and developed community projects.

Andrew Young was a top aide to Dr. Martin Luther King, Jr., during the civil rights movement. He helped found the Southern Christian Leadership Conference and served as vice president of the organization. An ordained minister and former pastor, he took the road less traveled by answering the Lord's call beyond the walls of the church building. As a result of this decision, he served two terms as mayor of Atlanta, Georgia, and three terms in the United States Congress and was an ambassador to the United Nations. The crowning glory of his public service thus far has been receiving a Presidential Medal of Freedom.

CONTENTS

Leadership
Bethel AME Church
Baltimore, Maryland

Discipleship
Oak Cliff Bible Fellowship
Dallas, Texas

Worship
First African Methodist Episcopal Church (FAME)
Los Angeles, California

Evangelism
Soul Factory
Forestville, Maryland

Family
Christian Stronghold Baptist Church
Philadelphia, Pennsylvania

Stewardship
New Birth Missionary Baptist
Lithonia, Georgia

Community
West Angeles Church of God in Christ
Los Angeles, California

Relationships
Long Reach Church of God
Columbia, Maryland

FOREWORD

It is easy for me to tout the strengths of the African-American church. My father was a Baptist preacher and actually was the pastor of three churches at one time. He was the pastor of a first-and-third-Sunday church, a second-and-fourth-Sunday church and a fifth-Sunday church. I spent my entire young life in an African-American church, and now I pastor a predominantly African-American congregation myself. I believe this gives me a unique perspective to comment on the impact of African-American churches.

Early in my life, I recognized that one of the most vibrant sectors of the Church in America is the African-American church. Research and statistical data further substantiate the fact that as a group, our mere existence in some way shows we have a vital role in our nation and world. Being in an environment not always conducive to our success forced the African-American church to serve as the hub, holding our communities together through relevant, impacting ministry.

While this is all very relevant and true, I feel this book points to a much greater aspect of the Kingdom. Unfortunately, the purpose of dividing the church along racial lines is necessary at times in order not to devalue or inflate the importance of one group or another. While our focus here may begin with high-impact African-American churches, it must end as a wake-up call for the entire Church. The Kingdom emphasis I see is that we can be more effective working together as an entity that crosses archaic, racial boundaries to truly impact the world. Christ is building His Church to fulfill His mandate. This Church is to function in unity and celebrate its unique diversity at the same time.

I applaud George Barna for his diligent work and research. Equally, I laud Dr. Harry Jackson for bringing to light the sometimes forgotten fact that we all are the Church, of which African-Americans are an equally vital part. As we recognize our individual, cultural and corporate significance in Christ, we can pour an undiluted gospel of Kingdom redemption into the world and make disciples of all peoples.

Bishop Eddie L. Long
Senior Pastor
New Birth Missionary Baptist Church
Lithonia, Georgia

PREFACE

It is such a joy to know and to be known by God. To have the opportunity to serve Him and His people through the creation of a book like this is an unwarranted privilege. We hope that you will find value in this work that will manifest itself in stronger and more vibrant personal and corporate ministry.

May this book inform, instruct and inspire you, regardless of the nature of your ministry or the color of your primary audience. And may God's kingdom be advanced through the blending of our research and your application of the findings. All that we do is for His glory and in His service.

Now, let's examine the heart and soul of the African-American church.

ACKNOWLEDGMENTS

No book is created in a vacuum. Both of the authors wish to express their gratitude to the myriad individuals who have played a significant role in the creation of this work.

FROM GEORGE BARNA

One of the conclusions I drew from the early research and feedback for this book was that an educated, evangelical, middle-class Caucasian (yup, that's me) can only develop so much insight into what it means to be an African-American Christian in (post)modern America. The research has produced a body of insights that I believe are useful for all Christians and all Christ-centered churches—but that may risk being "dissed" simply because the analysis is from a *white* sociologist. Even more important to me is the likelihood that my own experiences and innate biases might prevent me from learning and sharing significant insights.

By the grace of God, I came to know Bishop Harry Jackson. After a series of encounters, discussions and joint ministry ventures, we agreed to write this book together. I am honored to have been able to work on this book with one of the best and brightest pastors in America—not just a great *African-American* pastor, but a great *Christian* pastor. Harry has brought a wealth of experience in business, higher education and ministry to this project. As an intelligent and strategic leader, Harry threw himself into this book as a means of furthering his own growth as a follower of Christ, an African-American leader and a pastor—and as a means of contributing to the growth of the Christian

Church in this nation. His stellar efforts on this project have been an inspiration to me.

The Maclellan Foundation started this whole ball rolling by providing a grant to fund the initial research. Tom McCallie was a valuable sounding board and gave useful direction to the project. Hugh Maclellan, Jr., also added valuable wisdom and encouragement.

Kim Wilson initially became involved in this work as a friend interested in our work, then as a part-time consultant and finally as our marketing director. She provided invaluable insight and professional assistance in conducting the research and in marketing the project through our sister entity, The Barna Institute. Kim's experience as an African-American woman working with African-American churches throughout the Southeast added many hard-won insights into black spirituality and church culture. They don't come any better than Kim, and I will always be thankful for the role she played in guiding the project.

Also instrumental in the process were the directors of The Barna Group, through which this work was originally facilitated. That group included Bob Buford, Connie DeBord, Bill Greig III, Molly Davis Scott and Luder Whitlock. Their ideas, contacts and hands-on assistance were the foundation on which the project was built. Not only did they serve without pay but they also donated their professional expertise to launch this work.

My colleagues at The Barna Group have been continually supportive of my quirky leadership of our company as it has lurched to and fro, bouncing between research, consulting, coalition building, education, marketing and advertising, direct ministry, political influence and who knows what else. While they are too kind to say so, I'm sure this project seemed to emerge out of left field, but they stayed committed and focused, allowing us to produce something that will help people. My appreciation goes to Cameron Hubiak, Pam Jacob, David Kinnaman, Jill Kinnaman, Jamie McLaughlin and Celeste Rivera.

Gospel Light has been publishing books I have written for more than a decade. This one, more than most, is outside the boundaries of the typical ministry book. I appreciate their willingness to take on this challenge and to assume the financial risk of making the strategic intelligence gathered available to the wider Body of Christ. I want to acknowledge Bill Greig III for his personal passion for bringing the research results to the public's attention, for consistently investing in me as a person and as a servant of the Church and for teaming me with Harry Jackson for this project; Kyle Duncan, Deena Davis and Kim Bangs for their patience and guidance in the editorial process; and for the entire Regal Books team that labors behind the scenes to develop an idea expressed at a lunch meeting into a book that lands in bookstores, churches and households around the world.

Last but never least, I am so thankful for the love and support of my family. This is a project that began nearly a decade ago—and my girls have never failed to be there for me. My wife, Nancy, and my daughters, Samantha and Corban, have consistently and passionately prayed for me and for this book. These women of God are a special treasure to me.

FROM HARRY JACKSON

First of all, I thank the Lord Jesus Christ for the opportunity to coauthor this book with George Barna. The opportunity, in and of itself, has truly been a dream come true. George has long been one of my spiritual heroes, whose statistics I have relied upon for many years. Therefore, I was almost overwhelmed when Bill Greig III first recommended that George and I write this book together. Secondly, I would like to thank George for his openness and teamwork in finally bringing this book to the market. The two-year period that it has taken us to get from the idea stage to the bookstore has gone by relatively quickly because of his gracious and professional demeanor.

I want to echo George's thanks to all my friends at Regal. I also want to thank Jan Sherman who works with us at Hope Christian Church for overseeing the research team that assisted us in working through all the details of the leadership interviews and for the countless hours of writing and rewriting involved in this project.

Thanks also to the following people who helped Jan and me with research, editing or input: Keith Wall, Joni Jackson, Marcille Moss, Blessing Ogiata, Tina Green, Tyra Holland and Sherlita Queen.

I want to offer our appreciation to Bishop Eddie Long, Elder Tommy Powell and the staff of New Birth Missionary Baptist; Dr. Frank Reid, Leronia Josey and the staff of Bethel AME Church of Baltimore; Bishop Robert Davis, Pastor Suzanne Haley and the staff of Long Reach Church of God; Dr. Cecil L. Murray, Diane Young and the staff of First AME Church of Los Angeles; Pastor Deron Cloud and the staff of the Soul Factory; Bishop Charles E. Blake and the staff of West Angeles Church of God in Christ; Dr. Willie Richardson and the staff of Christian Stronghold Baptist Church; Dr. Tony Evans, Dr. Martin Hawkins and the staff of Oak Cliff Bible Fellowship for their help.

I want to thank my family: my wife, Michele, for her confidence in the destiny of this book; my daughters, Joni Michele and Elizabeth, must also be thanked because of the time I had to spend writing during several family holidays.

Last but not least, great thanks are due to the ministry team at Hope Christian Church. God has given me gracious staff, elders and congregants who have allowed me the time to write, research and develop the information included in these pages.

IS THERE REALLY ANYTHING THAT WHITE CHURCHES CAN LEARN FROM BLACK CHURCHES?

*Black preachers and white preachers have tended to minister in
isolation. . . . Church leaders and pastors need to become more
sensitive to the needs of people of other cultural backgrounds in order
to be able to lead the church effectively in a new century.*

—E. K. BAILEY AND WARREN WIERSBE

The title of this chapter sounds absurd, doesn't it? After all, we
all know that we are capable of learning profound lessons from
the most insignificant experiences. Certainly, then, we can discover deep truths and insights from the experience and practices
of black churches.

But, putting theory aside, the question remains: What have
you learned about transformational ministry through the experience and practices of black churches in America? Is the notion
of drawing compelling wisdom from their activity even on your
radar screen?

Some ministry leaders to whom we have mentioned this book—most of them white males—have given me a quizzical glance, as if their real question were why anyone would bother to examine the black population and its faith for clues that might strengthen Christ's Church in America. Our reaction is to pose a few questions for their reflection. Let us share a few of those with you.

Are you aware that black adults are more likely to be born-again Christians than white adults?

Do you know that when we tested 22 common goals that people pursue, the top-rated goal among black adults is to have

Are you aware that black adults are more likely to be born-again Christians than white adults?

a close relationship with God, while that same goal is ranked fifth by whites? Or that being actively involved in a church is a goal pursued by three-quarters of all black adults but by less than half of all white adults?

Would you be surprised to discover that black adults are nearly twice as likely as white adults to read the Bible during a typical week, other than when they are at church? Or that black adults are 50 percent more likely than white adults to strongly affirm that the Bible is totally accurate in everything it teaches?

Have you seen the recent research indicating that African-American adults are much more likely than whites, Hispanics or

Asians to discuss spiritual matters with other people?

Does it make sense to you that the typical African-American church raises more money for ministry each year than does the typical Caucasian church—despite the lower levels of household income and of membership in the black congregations?

Although white megachurches receive an extraordinary amount of media attention, do you know that there is a higher percentage of megachurches among black churches than among white churches?

The cumulative weight of these findings suggests that the black church is more than a knockoff of the white Protestant church in America. There is something truly spectacular taking place in the lives of millions of African-Americans and it has been ignited by the goings-on in their church.

As a Caucasian, I (George) have to admit that analyzing the results of a large body of research focused on the faith of the African-American community blew me away. Prior to the research I was aware of the obvious differences: black church music is more energetic and soulful, their preachers are often spellbinding orators, and their congregants get more dressed up for worship services than do most white folks. However, I was not at all prepared for the nature and magnitude of the substantive differences I discovered between the white and black segments of the United States.

When the research project that culminated in this book was initiated several years ago, I discussed the project with a number of publishers. The common—almost universal—reaction was to predict that the audience for a book about the faith lessons to be learned from studying African-Americans and their churches would be too small to justify publishing such a volume. Undeterred, we moved ahead and completed the research, produced a report and continued to update the information annually with the hope of eventually publishing the insights in book form.

During the ensuing years, many of my professional colleagues remained skeptical about the value of this project. Many questions have been asked about the wisdom of investing time, money and energy in studying the black population and its religious life. Let us explain why this work is just as important for you as it has been for us.

MOTIVATIONS REVEALED

For a quarter century, the surveys The Barna Group has conducted have consistently shown major differences in attitudes, beliefs and behaviors among blacks and America's other ethnic groups. One of the most overt distinctions relates to faith. A wide variety of measures indicate that black people turn to their faith for guidance more often than do other people and that their faith is more frequently Christian than any other alternative. Our studies have also consistently revealed that black people regard their church as a central element in their lives and that the pastor of that church is perhaps the single most important leader to whom they relate and from whom they are willing to take direction.

As a researcher and leader who longs to see the Christian faith taken more seriously in America, we sensed that there were clues to ministry efficacy to be gleaned from the experience of African-Americans. *Why is the Christian faith more real to this particular segment of the population than any other?*

In the regular course of our research, I (George) interview and analyze hundreds of black teenagers, adults, pastors and churches every year. My visceral experience verified the statistical insights that were evident: Black people seemed to know, experience and relate to God in ways very different from those of whites, Hispanics and Asians. Their music, prayers, sermons, applications drawn from Bible study and even their socializing exhibited unique style and flair. While some of the differences were consistent with stereotypes I had been exposed to since my earliest years, many of their behaviors and perspectives bore no resemblance to those ingrained expectations. *What would happen if we could eliminate our predispositions and understand the black faith experience for what it is—that is, if we could see the reality without expectations and prejudices affecting our vision? What could the rest of us learn from an ethnic group that has endured incredible persecution and hardship without blaming God for their difficulties?*

One of the most puzzling realities has been that when The Barna Group contacted religious institutions—denominations, in particular—and asked for examples of churches that were doing excellent work in a particular field of ministry (e.g., worship, evangelism, community service), it was rare for a black congregation to be identified. One way of getting around that problem, of course, would be to get additional recommendations from denominations that are predominantly, if not exclusively, black; e.g., African Methodist Episcopal (AME), African Methodist Episcopal (AME) Zion, Church of God in Christ (COGIC), Missionary Baptist, National Baptist. However, despite repeated attempts over many different projects, we found it virtually impossible to get assistance from those organizations. Consequently, we had to work much harder to find examples of black churches that were—and are—doing a great job—these churches exist but they tend to remain below the radar screen of the white ministry establishment, the mass media and academicians who study ministry activity. *What treasures and insights are we missing because of the segre-*

gation and isolation that characterize the Church world in the United States? What might be gained by giving various black churches their due by recognizing their superb ministry efforts and the lessons they have learned through their experience?

Indeed, in the professional circles I (George) travel within—mostly white, Protestant and evangelical—there is a desire to learn and grow. Yet there is also a strange tendency to keep seeking new insights from the same sources, returning to the same well over and over, hoping that further dredging will supply pristine breakthroughs. While there are one or two churches each year that are added to the queue of those from which "new" knowledge is discovered, these churches are generally no more than 10 degrees different from the predecessor models. There seems to be some reluctance to expand the circle of sources from which we might draw inspiration, insight and instruction. *As great as they are, can we continue to behave as if Willow Creek and Saddleback are the only churches that have figured out how to do effective ministry? Are the pastors of suburban megachurches like these the sole proprietors of ministry wisdom? If the desire of so many churches is to work "outside the box," then isn't it reasonable to think that black churches may be working within a different box? Just as American churches drew ministry principles from the revivals in Argentina and South Korea a decade ago, isn't it reasonable to believe that the churches within our own culture that have developed the strongest ties with people might have some compelling revelations for the bulk of the nation's ministries?*

The media, the national filter through which most people derive their perspectives and values, live on anecdotes. Their stock-in-trade is to find one or two interesting examples of a behavior or a viewpoint, conduct a few interviews, add some personal observations and announce the discovery of a trend. Coverage of the religious scene is no different. Christian and secular journalists alike tend to pounce on singular experiences and approaches as models that are the harbingers of the future. In recent years, dissecting the genius of megachurches has been the rage among religious journalists. Yet, once again, black megachurches are frequently overlooked—even though there is a higher percentage of large black congregations than there is among white or Hispanic congregations. In fact, while Willow Creek and Saddleback are regularly touted by the media as the biggest churches in North America, there are at least a dozen black churches whose attendance exceeds either of those well-known congregations by at least a couple thousand people per week! *What are the dynamics of these behemoth African-American congregations? Is it more than just the world-class oratory of the preachers or the talent of the gospel choirs? Are there some crosscultural principles to be derived from those ministries?*

One of the trends that we have witnessed in the past decade has been increased interest in developing multicultural churches. This is partly in response to the ethnic diversification of the country's population, thanks largely to immigration, partly a response to the ardent desire of the two youngest generations to destroy the racial boundaries that continue to make Sunday mornings the most segregated time of the week and partly due to the heightened theological sensitivity to the inappropriateness of having churches that are ethnically uniform. Our studies note that the interest has resulted in limited growth in the number of multicultural congregations—and that much of the resistance is attributable to the fact that people do not really want to lose the comfort and security represented by their style of ministry. *Before we make a headlong leap into intentional multiethnic congregations, are there still additional insights to be drawn from unicultural congregations that might eventually lead to more effective and organic multicultural ministries? Rather than forcing people together on the basis of skin color, because it seems like the right thing to do, are there ministry distinctives that must be comprehended and integrated into a multicultural setting for it to be healthy and lasting?*

Finally, we want to describe the black faith experience if for no other reason than because of the magnitude and significance of the black population. The United States has as many African-Americans as there are people living in California—close to 40 million individuals. That segment will increase by another 5 million people by 2010. *As perhaps the single most cohesive and solidly committed block of Christians in our nation, why not provide resources that will help black churches and ministries to better understand their culture, their people and their ministry impact?*

Conducting such research seems like a no-lose deal. Everyone involved in ministry could learn significant insights from studying black churches and the faith of black individuals more closely. If we are truly a unified Church, rather than a collection of isolated churches each looking out for themselves, then such an effort will help all of us recognize what God is doing through and among one particular group within the larger body of believers. Rather than viewing this research as marginal or esoteric, as some characterized the concept, we believe it represents a useful addition to the aggregate understanding we share regarding ministry dynamics and the opportunities for Christianity to be a truly transforming faith.

PROCESS CLARIFIED

The research for this book began in earnest in 1996, sparked by a generous financial gift from the Maclellan Foundation. After reading some 30 books on the black experience in America, I (George) developed a list of experts who seemed capable of pointing me in the right direction at the start of this project. Through The Barna Group, we then interviewed two dozen

experts regarding African-American lifestyles, faith and churches, seeking to develop sufficient expertise even to know what to
look for as we rolled out the research. Subsequently, we conducted three nationwide surveys among African-American
adults (800 telephone interviews, lasting approximately 20 minutes each), among senior pastors of black churches (400 telephone interviews, lasting approximately 18 minutes each) and
among black teenagers (254 telephone interviews, lasting
approximately 16 minutes each). That research, conducted in
1996, has been supplemented by a series of national telephone
surveys among black adults, teenagers and pastors each year
since 1996, with smaller samples of those target audiences
involved. (The average number of completed surveys among
black adults has been in the 400-600 range each year, approximately 60-100 black pastors each year and roughly 75-100 black
teenagers each year.)

The framework for analysis that has been used is based on
the work that was released in my book *The Habits of Highly Effective
Churches*, which was a long-term study of certain churches (mostly, but not exclusively, white) and what enabled them to be effective in ministry. In that project we learned that effective churches
develop a series of habits that facilitate life transformation. The
habits are typically found in relation to nine areas of activity:

1. Facilitating genuine and regular worship of God
2. Providing intentional and strategic spiritual formation activities
3. Empowering individuals to "live evangelistically"
4. Serving the community with consistency, excellence
   and humility
5. Motivating and teaching people to be good stewards
   of every resource God has provided them

6. Developing relationships among believers in which they are spiritually accountable to each other

7. Providing strong, visionary, faith-driven leadership to the congregation

8. Building up families to be the faith center of each person's life

9. Creating structures and procedures that facilitate growing, healthy ministry

This research was built upon that same framework with a sensitivity to the potential of finding additional avenues of strength that enable black churches to be vibrant.

Throughout the text you will see us use the terms "black" and "African-American" interchangeably. Understandably, some individuals assign different meaning to each of these terms. In this exchange of ideas, however, we have chosen to use these terms without distinction. We have avoided the use of "Pan African" specifically because of its divergent connotations. It is not our intent to be offensive or simplistic but rather to communicate in ways that will resonate with our readers.

WHOLENESS RESTORED

So, what you are about to read is a decade-long journey of discovery that blends research facts, qualitative analysis and personal experience drawn from various quarters. To some, the constant return to black history may seem irrelevant; to African-Americans, that history is still very real and significant. Some readers may consider the various insights described to be strangely new, wondering why these discoveries have not been made public before. It is a good question, one that challenges our claim of being a body of believers united in Christ.

Most of all, however, we hope you are ready to learn some practical and helpful insights about yourself, your ministry, the portion of the culture you connect with and portions of our society that have remained shrouded in mystery to you. I (George) will be the first to confess that I knew relatively little about ministry in black America before this study—and that I am much better off for having taken this journey.

We hope to portray the robust ministry presence and influence of the nation's black churches as they facilitate spiritual transformation in millions of lives. There are lessons to be learned by all churches and their leaders, regardless of the racial and ethnic segmentation of their own congregation. May this journey enable all of us truly to become the one, holy and universal Church that Jesus died to restore to wholeness.

CHAPTER 1

FAITH AMONG BLACK AMERICANS

True faith is never merely a source of spiritual comfort. It may indeed bring peace, but before it does so it must involve us in struggle period. A "faith" that avoids this struggle is really a temptation against true faith.
—THOMAS MERTON

Researchers frequently go to great lengths to point out the differences among population segments. We know, for instance, that there are huge gaps in values, attitudes and behaviors across generations. We have learned that men and women are wired so differently that some people are not sure the two genders come from the same solar system! Racial and ethnic background is another source of distinction, as is a person's geographic location. It is common for researchers to analyze survey data according to 60 or more different subgroups of the population, searching for the patterns that enable us to understand people better and predict their behavior.

But in the end, all of that digging for differences masks one unavoidable truth: People are people. One of the remarkable outcomes that has emerged from the more than 100,000 personal interviews The Barna Group has conducted over the last two decades is how *similar* people are in their perspectives on life, regardless of their socioeconomic or ethnic background. Upon revisiting thousands of interviews in order to assess the similarities and differences between blacks and whites in America, there is at least one inescapable conclusion that must be drawn: There are many more areas of similarity than uniqueness among the American people.

There is a ratio of nearly six white people to every black person in the United States but our studies showed that whites and blacks talk about the same topics with their friends.

This conclusion was front and center in our minds as we analyzed the statistics portraying the lives of whites and blacks in this country. There is a ratio of nearly six white people to every black person in the United States but our studies showed that whites and blacks talk about the same topics with their friends.[1] They endure the same pressures from day to day—busy schedules, fractured relationships and career challenges.[2] People describe the same types and magnitude of emotional ups and downs in the roller coaster of life.[3] Americans, regardless of their color, make many good choices—and, unfortunately, many bad ones too. In the end, people do the best they can to make sense out of life, to enjoy each new day and to achieve success based upon whatever criteria they have devised.

In spite of the general resemblance of our lives, our research discerned some areas in which whites and blacks are clearly divergent. For instance, black adults are more likely to struggle with finances and substance abuse.[4] They often labor through feelings of loneliness and a sense of disconnection from other people.[5] (This is especially true for black men.) They also are very vulnerable to sexual temptations, whether that takes the form of physical intimacy with a nonspouse or enjoyment of pornographic materials.[6] In fact, family realities become a point of confusion and stress for millions of blacks—they are nearly twice as likely as whites never to get married and are more than twice as likely to have a child out of wedlock.[7] Although black Americans recognize the importance of family and attribute their personal strength and success in large measure to what they absorbed from their family experience, millions of blacks admit that the typical black family is dysfunctional or a source of conflict rather than safety and security.[8]

African-Americans experience a score of different emotional reactions to life too. For instance, we discovered that black adults and teenagers are more likely than their white counterparts to feel misunderstood by other people and to contend that their anger or inappropriate words get them into irreconcilable difficulties.[9] A huge majority of blacks argue that they deserve to experience a better quality of life; perhaps that explains why blacks are more likely than any other ethnic group in America to describe themselves as "totally committed to getting ahead in life."[10]

Unexpectedly, we found that black adults are substantially more likely than white adults to say that their careers come before anything else in their lives. This might relate to the facts that blacks have the lowest average household income of any ethnic group, the highest rate of poverty and the highest proportion of unemployed individuals. In this, the land of opportunity, we discovered a variety of factors indicating that black adults are not willing to accept poverty and second-class status in America.

Life remains a bit of a mystery for millions of black citizens. For instance, a majority of them admit that they are still seeking clarity regarding the purpose and meaning of their lives.[11] They also perceive race relations in the nation to be continually deteriorating, making their emphasis upon social parity and family comfort more tenuous.[12] Perhaps this is why a large share of blacks acknowledge that they are "concerned about the future"—not so much from a sociopolitical perspective as from a personal, survival viewpoint.[13]

COPING MECHANISMS

Given the character and magnitude of the pressures and challenges we face every day, each of us must develop a series of coping mechanisms. We have observed that there are ethnic patterns related to how people handle their struggles. For example, the primary coping mechanism for most white Americans relates to the development and deployment of marketplace abilities and rewards. The more they are able to learn that will advance their standing in the marketplace and the more occupational skills they master, the more money they are capable of earning, which produces esteem, self-confidence, security and comfort.

Hispanics in the United States approach life differently. They cope with life's tensions primarily by relying upon the strength derived from family cohesion. By giving and receiving love within the nuclear and extended family, Hispanics achieve their sense of identity and stability.

Blacks have yet a different coping mechanism: reliance on their faith. Drawing strength from the Bible and from their relationship with God, African-Americans are more likely than other people to view their lives as a gift from God and to view God as their sustainer in all circumstances. They seek guidance in life through the tools of their faith—prayer, Scripture, Bible teaching and spiritual counsel. They are the ethnic group most fervent in claiming the promises of God for personal endurance and perseverance in life. While family is usually not seen as the dominant place of refuge and community, church is; and whereas their jobs rarely offer the hope and encouragement to sustain them in tough times, their faith provides that and more.[14]

They are not faultless or pure, but millions of American blacks view material success as a bonus tacked on to the eternal rewards provided by God.

In essence, the Promised Land sought by whites in this country is material success. Obtaining the proverbial pot of gold at the end of the rainbow is the treasure that whites are most deeply devoted to claiming. For blacks, however, the Promised Land is the rainbow itself, reflecting their understanding that the rainbow is God's sign that He will never wash away His people (see Gen. 9:13-16). In practical terms, blacks rely on their acceptance by, the presence of and the wisdom they derive from God as their coping tools. They are not faultless or pure, but millions of American blacks view material success as a bonus tacked on to the eternal rewards provided by God to those who love Him and strive to live according to His ways.

CENTRALIZED FAITH

As you will discover in subsequent chapters of this book, the widespread reliance of blacks on their faith in God is no accident. There are four complementary streams of training that have reinforced the centrality of Christianity in the lives of black Americans.

1. Seeking the Source

Blacks have been driven by their daily experiences to search for something that would enable them to transcend the pain and hopelessness that they have so often encountered in the United States. Blacks have endured racial prejudice in myriad forms for more than two centuries, resulting in economic, physical, educational, spiritual, political and legal limitations. They have been exposed to injustice in every corner of society, from laws that have promoted inequalities to the unfair application of just laws.

All of these experiences have driven them to seek a source of strength and power that would enable them to bear daily hardships. Most Americans have turned inward, seeking to draw upon an inner reservoir of courage and determination to overcome whatever seeks to hinder or oppress them. Blacks, for the most part, have turned upward, placing themselves at God's mercy and accepting their earthly fate as part of a preparation process for eternity. Drawing upon hard-earned faith-based lessons, they realize that no human being can make it alone; all human strength and authority is derived, and the source is God Himself. Blacks are generally willing to acknowledge their weakness and to draw from Him as their source.

2. Handing Down Traditions

The black religious experience is partially a result of traditions handed down over many years through black culture. The symbols, language and values that are at the heart of black culture come largely from the spiritual underpinnings they share. Much like the tribes of Israel and the early Christians who transmitted their faith to subsequent generations through verbal expressions, the African-American experience is largely an oral rather than a written tradition. Many of the customs and views that are ingrained in that subculture can be traced to spiritual origins that have been passed along through family conversations, mentoring and Church-based teaching.

3. Extending Community

American blacks are the most comfortable with the African proverb "It takes a village to raise a child." This philosophy may be a residue from the days when most blacks were slaves living on plantations; women not only cared for their own children while the men were at work but also raised children whose parents had died prematurely. That same mentality—that black people are an extended community—is evident in the child-rearing practices of so many unwed African-American women whose children are brought up by their mothers, grandmothers and other kinfolk. The hub of activity and encouragement for these divergent family forms is their church. Their common bond—skin color, shared faith and oppressed social standing—has long served as the thread that weaves them together.

4. Partnering with the Church

Christianity has taken center stage in the lives of most blacks because they were raised through a partnership of their mother and their church. This statement is not to discredit the role of black men, it simply reflects the sentiments of the African-American community itself. Most blacks admit that their primary nurturing—philosophical, physical, moral and spiritual—came from their mother.[15] Mothers give credit to their church family for providing advice, encouragement and material assistance. It is a partnership driven by the mother but fortified by the church.

INTEGRATED LIFE

Christianity has become an unquestioned foundation of the black lifestyle after many decades of their having integrated faith and life. In fact, this unchallenged marriage of blacks and Christianity is what has made the recent interest in Islam among some blacks (especially males) so noteworthy.

In our pluralist society the real wonder is not that some blacks have embraced Islam but that so few have done so. One reason that blacks are less likely to be atheistic or to embrace a faith other than Christianity is that faith in Christ has served the black community well. Perhaps more than any other people group in America's history, blacks can relate to the life of Christ—the suffering servant, the hard-working craftsman whose skills were challenged, the gentle spirit who courageously defended the weak and the rejected.

There are various reasons why African-Americans have clung to the Christian faith even when other faiths and worldviews have gained favor with the rest of the nation's population. As we will discuss, most blacks believe that every word in the Bible is true and trustworthy but very few of them possess a complete biblical worldview.[16] This is similar to the situation among white, Hispanic and Asian Christians living in the United States. But blacks have gone farther down the road of spiritual integration, developing their life philosophy around biblical principles and themes. Their faith in Jesus Christ has become the ultimate safety net for them, providing a powerful means of understanding the tragedies and disappointments of life even if their theology is not fully defensible on biblical grounds.

Because their faith is so central to their comprehension of and response to life's circumstances, blacks treat their faith as an infallible source of comfort rather than as a compartment of activity or information that must be activated at certain times of the week (e.g., Sunday morning). Whereas our research suggests that whites and Asians, in particular, have failed to integrate their faith into the varied dimensions of their lives, blacks have shown a tendency to introduce elements of their faith into every dimension of their lives. This capacity to introduce faith principles into their relationships, occupational efforts, finances, community involvement and parenting has enabled millions of black individuals to handle otherwise intolerable or impossible situations.

This might be explained by recognizing that blacks view their faith as a relationship with God rather than as a system of thought and beliefs. Whites are prone to memorize and recite Bible verses as a demonstration of religious knowledge. Blacks tend to remember Bible verses as a means of comfort and guidance during trials and tribulations. The bottom line is that blacks treat life as a faith-based work in progress while whites more commonly see the content of their faith as a product they have achieved. Blacks see life as a faith-based journey, whereas whites see faith as a series of interrelated destinations they might arrive at if they work at it hard enough.

Different Approaches

Interestingly, our nation's churches have facilitated these different approaches to faith development. Consider how churches operate.

White churches define large numbers of attenders as the mark of success. In order to appeal to increasing numbers of people, white churches generally attempt to read the culture and then contextualize their ministry so as to be seen as relevant and valuable. The teaching in white churches typically focuses on how Scripture enables us to live effectively within our culture—never compromising scriptural principles but always seeking ways of blending faith and lifestyle into a mix that is palatable to God.

Black churches define social influence as the mark of success. Instead of accepting society for what it is and figuring out how to accommodate the culture, the sign of leadership is providing a Scripture-based alternative to what the prevailing culture is offering. The teaching in black churches tends to emphasize inner strength in the midst of struggle, emotional and spiritual trust in the midst of isolation, endurance in the midst of long-term hardship, and joy in the midst of deprivation and humiliation. If white churches typically teach people how to make the most of any situation, black churches often emphasize how to overcome any situation. While most white churches focus on the here and now, most black churches remind their people that the hereafter is where the real action is.

This very different viewpoint is reflected in the life goals of whites and blacks. Whites are most interested in developing relationships with people, achieving personal success and enjoying material comfort. Blacks are more interested in their relationship with God, societal influence and emotional security.[17] These leanings underscore that whites want to make the most of their time on Earth; blacks want to live appropriately here so that they can maximize their post-Earth experience.

Whereas white adults emphasize the importance of education for getting ahead, black adults focus on faith for perspective and endurance. Blacks are increasingly desirous of higher incomes and better quality of life, but they usually strive to satisfy such goals in harmony with their spiritual perspectives. While most whites derive their self-esteem from their personal accomplishments and their potential to achieve, blacks seek their esteem from their spiritual resolve reinforced by family and church-based relationships. The themes that power white ascendancy in the marketplace—"it's who you know that counts," "the Rolodex is the modern-day Bible of choice" and the current emphasis upon networking—are countered by the black community's turning to the local church for its own infusion of

> *Black pastors see politics as the means of making faith real by introducing faith principles into every fiber of life.*

power through shared family experience, the provision of material support for members in need and the emotional encouragement to face another week of the world's challenges.

Perhaps it is in the pastorate that black and white faith differences are most clear. White pastors most frequently see themselves as facilitators of individual spiritual growth within a loosely managed communal context. Black pastors see themselves as the power brokers of black influence in a white society, relying upon the uncontested support of their congregation as well as their personal spiritual strength and principles to guide their efforts. With some notable exceptions, white pastors avoid politics like the plague; amazingly few sermons overtly address current political issues and surprisingly few white congregations have any noticeable presence in the political arena. In contrast, black pastors see politics as the means of making faith real by introducing faith principles into every fiber of life. As the marketplace gladiators representing black interests, African-American pastors naturally relate their ministry to every social issue pertinent to the day. White pastors who make similar efforts are often castigated by their congregants and other white clergy who find their actions inappropriate.

Church life is changing dramatically in all of the ethnic sectors of society. One of the areas that has changed little in recent years, however, is the gap between how much time blacks and whites spend at church. The idea of a Sabbath still resonates within the black culture; this concept was lost more than a quarter century ago in white America. The typical black church service lasts longer, black people spend more time on the church campus socializing after their services, and Sunday-evening services remain more common in black congregations than in white churches. These lasting trends are a sign that the spiritual focus remains paramount among blacks.

Church Strategy

To provide blacks with a faith that permeates every dimension of life, black churches are more likely than others to weave the various aspects of ministry into a seamless experience. Blacks spend much more time at church than do whites because the experience they receive is more central to their lives. Even though their congregants are not as well-off financially, black churches raise more money per capita than do others because their congregants see their church as a necessary extension of their life, not merely a worthy organization to which they feel some limited allegiance. The plans put forth by the pastor of black churches are followed with limited discussion or dissension because blacks view the church as a place subject to God-ordained authority rather than a democracy in which even the rules of conduct are negotiable.

Most churches, regardless of the racial or ethnic groups they serve, struggle to develop a healthy, holistic ministry that continually honors God. As a human expression of faith, the local church invariably reflects the imperfections of those who lead it and populate it. The study of thousands of churches over the years has made it evident that there is no perfect church to be found this side of heaven. But it is just as obvious that there are many vibrant and healthy churches whose people are helping God's kingdom to advance in spectacular ways. What is it that enables a church to become one of those stellar representatives of the Kingdom?

CHAPTER 2

BLACK CHURCH LEADERSHIP

Good leaders make people feel that they're at the very heart of things,
not at the periphery. Everyone feels that he or she makes a difference to
the success of the organization. When that happens, people feel centered
and that gives their work meaning.

—WARREN BENNIS

One of the most startling impressions left on white pastors after visiting black churches is the degree of respect and deference given to the black pastor. In most white congregations, the pastor is appreciated and listened to but is clearly seen as a hired hand responsible for providing vision to the lay leaders and congregants who then make the final decisions and implement plans. In contrast, the senior pastor is clearly "da man" in the typical black church.[1] He is given authority, expected to use it and counted upon by congregants to take the church where it otherwise would not go.

Why is there such a huge difference in how churches treat their leaders? One reason relates to the fact that African-

Americans regard their pastor as the single most important leader they follow. Aware of the challenges they face in life and cognizant that their ultimate reward will come after they die rather than during their earthly existence, blacks rely upon their pastor to represent them to the outside world. More than political officials, business executives or any other people of position or influence, the pastor is called upon to express their interests and to bring the authority of God to the battlefield of ideas and power. As a result, black pastors are given much more leeway in their schedule, spending and strategic thinking.

The senior pastor is clearly "da man" in the typical black church.

Further, black adults tend to see their relationship with their pastor as a partnership. Hoping for progress in race relations, economic opportunities, educational reform, lifestyle enhancement and political authority as well as in spiritual growth, blacks recognize that their leader is only as effective as his followers are committed to following through on the vision, strategies and tactics that he has laid out. Whereas white pastors often find their leadership occurs in an adversarial environment, black pastors find their leadership occurs in an environment that is more acquiescent but often also has a greater sense of investment in the ultimate outcomes.

If white churches develop a partnership involving lay leaders, congregants and the pastor, that unity often comes only after the pastor has passed the test and given evidence of vision and leadership prowess. In black churches, the formula is different: The pastor is given the reigns from day one and expected to perform in concert with his people, losing that confidence only if the early returns indicate that he is incapable of fostering congregational unity and positive change in lives and society.

This intentional partnership in the black church stems from the notion that effective leadership results from balancing authority and democracy. Rather than asserting his rights as an autocratic leader, an effective black pastor strikes a healthy balance between calling the shots and giving congregants a substantial stake and role in the ministry. When Reverend Elliot Mason was asked whether the ideal condition is having a strong pastor or a strong democracy, he noted:

> It is not a question of either/or, but both/and. A strong pastor maintains democracy. He keeps things in order, minimizes power, maintains democracy. He keeps things in order, minimizes power grabs, maintains the balance of power. When someone on a board calls the pastor a dictator, it simply means that the pastor is keeping that person or board from dictating.[2]

This degree of interdependence and trust is exemplified by the experience of one of the nation's black megachurches. The pastor assumed his role after the church had gone several years without a full-time pastor. The deacons had done their best to lead the church during the interim period while the congregation prayed for and waited on God to supply the right senior leader. Upon assuming the post, the pastor was the beneficiary of strong lay leadership that welcomed him to the head position. "As soon as they called me to serve in that great office, the rules changed," the pastor recalled. "[The head deacon] repeatedly told church members and other leaders that the will of the pastor must be the will of the church."

This story illustrates one of the ways honor is given to black pastors. The deacons and department leaders of this established, traditional church had learned to work well without a senior pastor but the head deacon understood the need for a structural hierarchy and the visionary input of the senior leader. This deacon was a servant-hearted leader who challenged staff and lay leaders not to treat the young, inexperienced pastor as a novice employee. Built into their biblical and church leadership philosophy was the appropriateness of giving deference to the pastor's calling, vision and gifts. That deference did not imply that they expected flawless perfection or that they would give him blind obedience. It simply meant that they were willing to follow. They were encouraging him to set a visionary direction for the church in collaboration with them. From a biblical perspective their approach was similar to that of Joshua's followers who said, "Just as we fully obeyed Moses, so we will obey you" (Josh. 1:17).

To understand why African-American churches are comfortable placing their future in the hands of their pastors, you have to understand the role of the Church in black history.

A BRIEF HISTORY AND PERSPECTIVE

In keeping with African tradition, the pastor is seen as a tribal leader. Therefore, the pastor fills the role of a father regardless of his age. As a chieftain, he leads his people in their fight against evil. In pre-Civil War days, the church and the preacher were involved in the struggle for freedom from slavery. Some black scholars assert that after the Civil War preachers acclimated themselves to the culture and to their new freedoms; they lost that fierce, vigilant spirit that had maintained the focus and intensity of the black community for so long.

During the civil rights era, the countless stories of race-based injustice stirred the hearts of black church leaders to respond to their world as protective tribal chiefs. Yet there emerged a dimension of the Old Testament prophetic ministry as well. Prophets addressed the social conditions of Israel and Judah with clear words from God. They challenged God's people to live in a manner consistent with God's Word. Their message was always a call to return to the ways of God. The Old Testament prophets, though not always popular, were expected to speak the truth. Similarly, black preachers have often become oracles of truth and justice. Martin Luther King, Jr.'s letter from the Birmingham jail carried a certain prophetic authority, which pricked America's conscience. While Dr. King is the most widely remembered of the civil rights leaders, there were hundreds of other black pastors who were deeply and courageously involved in affecting the moral and spiritual nature of the country.

The civil rights movement during the '50s, '60s and '70s produced many individuals who emerged from within the Church at strategic times to become catalysts for social change. These previously unknown folks took to heart the haunting question posed by Mordecai to his niece Esther:

Who knows? Perhaps you have come to royal dignity for just such a time as this (Esther 4:14, NRSV).

They perceived the need for change and decided to step up to the plate by working closely with the recognized leaders of their world—pastors.

These nascent, often reluctant leaders were coached and

directed by black clergy who helped give them a platform. One such story is that of Mamie Till Bradley. Her son was tragically murdered during a summer vacation to Mississippi. Emmett Till was just 14 years old at the time of his death. Born in Chicago, he had been shielded from racism by his mother. His personal relationships were very innocent and uncomplicated.

As he bragged about his white girlfriends and his northern life, Emmett's Mississippi peers challenged him to prove that he was telling the truth. In a childish response to the playful taunting of his friends, he decided to flirt with a white female cashier in a local store. As Emmett left the tiny country store, he let out a wolf whistle. This act, innocent by northern standards, brought down the wrath of the tiny community's leaders. A few days later, two white men appeared at the house where Emmett was staying. They took him from his uncle's house, who happened to be a pastor, despite the family's cries for mercy. Emmett was pistol-whipped and beaten beyond recognition. His dead body was thrown off of the Tallahatchie Bridge on August 28, 1955.

When the badly decomposed corpse of this young man was presented to the local coroner, he could not tell whether the body was that of a black or white man. After he examined the body carefully, the coroner decided to permanently seal Emmett's casket shut.

Instead of being overwhelmed by her own tragedy, Mamie decided that her son's death would not be in vain. She and her courageous pastor, J. C. Williams of Robert Temple Church, made several decisions that would eventually change American history. First, they conferred with civil rights leaders to develop a wise plan of action. Next, they decided to reopen Emmett's casket for the funeral. Mamie emotionally declared, "The world must see what they did to my boy."[3]

Why an open casket? Most of the civil rights leaders of that day were ministers who believed that average Americans were good-hearted and that the power of the Holy Spirit would convict them of the sin of injustice. Their strategy worked. An estimated 125,000 people came to view the decayed and maimed body. *Life* magazine carried the confessions of the murderers, whom their fellow Mississippians refused to convict. Seven years

Why an open casket?

later, Bob Dylan immortalized Emmett's story in song.[4] Many people believe that Mamie Till Bradley's courageous act sparked the beginning of the modern civil rights movement.

This story is a classic example of how black laity and clergy have traditionally worked together toward common and significant goals. The laity would seek the counsel and assistance of their ministers. The clergy, in turn, would respond as servant leaders, focused on blending biblical principles with individual responsiveness and social action to produce positive transformation. The outgrowth of many years of selfless service is the respect and esteem granted to black pastors that enable them to continue in their drive to facilitate changed lives and a better society.

SOME LEADERSHIP STRUGGLES AND FOUNDATIONS

Most black churches experience one problem that plagues churches of all races and backgrounds: pastors who have not been called by God to be leaders. Our research indicates that among black pastors, only one out of every five claims to be gifted in areas such as leadership and administration—a proportion similar to that associated with other Protestant churches. In saying this we are making a distinction between holding a position of leadership and being called and gifted by God to be a leader. Having a degree in leadership, a desire to lead or even receiving positive feedback from others does not make a person a leader. Only God has the ability to make someone a leader, and even then that individual is responsible for refining the gifts and talents that have been bestowed upon him or her in order to lead at the highest possible level of competence.

True leaders are individuals who are called by God to give direction to His people and who have character that reflects His nature and standards as well as competencies that facilitate the accomplishment of progress for the Kingdom. These individuals are able to motivate people to rise above their circumstances and limitations and to focus on what really matters, to mobilize people around a set of desired outcomes, to help people accumulate the human, physical and financial resources required to accomplish the designated tasks, and to direct people toward the compelling and unique vision that God has reserved for that group of believers. In essence, leaders help people make sense of the existing reality and then to alter that reality to come into closer alignment with the reality that most honors and blesses God. God conveys that different reality through the vision He imparts to His leaders.

The effective black churches of our nation invariably have a true leader at the helm. But as we also find in studying other types of churches, the presence of a true leader is a necessary but insufficient condition for efficacy in ministry. These leaders leave their mark on individual lives and on society because of the way in which they involve and facilitate the effectiveness of those to whom they minister. In short, there are nine specific strategies that enable pastors to direct a life-changing ministry.

1. The Pastor as an Agent of Change

The typical black pastor is acutely aware of the respect and honor that his role carries. He realizes that he is the primary change agent for his church. Like our nation's president, the pastor in this setting has both policy-making and veto power. And while the pastor's role as the primary vision caster in the church is unchallenged, he is not allowed to operate as a tyrant. Black people want their church to be a place of safety from the oppressive ways of tyrants; the community of faith is designed to be an alternative to the untenable structures that have caused suffering and hardship for black people outside of the church.

The most effective black pastors recognize that their greatest influence in the church comes when they demonstrate the power of a godly model. The apostle Paul gave Timothy this advice in the Scriptures:

> Set an example for the believers in speech, in life, in love, in faith and in purity. Do not neglect your gift, which was given you through a prophetic message when the body of elders laid their hands on you (1 Tim. 4:12,14).

Toward that end, effective black pastors know that they must live a different kind of life. Their people look to them for clues as to what a transformed life looks like in a place that has often been inhospitable or unwelcoming. Just as God embraces leaders whose godly character shines through in the performance of their duties, so do God's people rely on their pastors to exemplify a holy life. This challenges pastors to demonstrate a relentless commitment to personal growth, both as a means of deepening their own relationship with God and as a way of coaching congregants to a greater Christlikeness.

In healthy congregations you will find overt support for believers who are struggling with the journey to become more like Jesus. Acknowledging that one's commitment to the process of transformation may be even more important to God than the product of such efforts, these pastors are surprisingly transparent about their own struggles with temptation and comfort. Such vulnerability builds a closer bond between the congregation and the pastor because he seems more human to them, while it also subtly motivates people to recognize and commit to the importance of the struggle to be a new person in Christ.

The emphasis on personal and societal change also explains why these black churches orient their preaching and teaching toward the application of biblical principles rather than simply identifying and explaining those admonitions. As primary purveyors of the concept that the role of the church is to comfort the afflicted and afflict the comfortable, effective churches generally examine conditions as opportunities for change. The pastors in black churches embrace their role in facilitating people's evolution as disciples of Jesus.

2. Communication That Inspires

Think about what it must be like to live in a world in which everyone knows you are different. One look at the color of your skin and the difference is apparent. Sometimes speech patterns betray the differences. For some, dress styles, poor physical health, the lack of educational achievements and even one's address are signs of being different. Keep in mind that such differences are often treated not simply as curiosities or signs of individuality but as reasons for fear, distrust, misunderstanding or even hatred.

Now consider your role as a leader of such people. Immediately you can sense the necessity and significance of lifting the spirits of these people. And that is why so many black pastors have honed their speaking skills, recognizing the need to lift up the downtrodden as well as the responsibility to represent their people eloquently to non-black audiences and influencers. The ability to motivate black people to see themselves as God sees them and to get them to reach for the dreams that God has for them has long been a vital dimension of black leadership.

There is great confusion in the Church world today: Most clergy believe that the key to being an effective pastor is the ability to persuasively present biblical truths in a logical, professionally presented half-hour sermon. Perhaps that is why so few churches are making a difference in our society or seeing many people live transformed, God-honoring lives. Churches are striving to change the world by telling stories rather than leading change. There is a lesson to be learned from great black leaders who know from experience that it is not enough just to be right or to be strategic. To make a difference, a leader must be a compelling advocate of a better life to the extent that people who have nothing left to give are willing to reach deep into their souls to find the will to persevere and then to prevail.

3. Leadership in a Team Context

As a group, black churches are the best in the land at team-based leadership. Many observers have erroneously attributed this to the close-knit community that is said to exist among African-Americans. Strangely, our data have consistently shown that if that camaraderie existed in the black community in decades past, it is no longer evident today. Family mobility, lifestyle fragmentation, isolation driven by mass media entertainment and the competitiveness of our social and economic networks have negatively affected the natural bond that black people used to enjoy.

Nevertheless, we found that the best of the nation's African-American religious bodies rely heavily on leadership by teams rather than the outstanding gifts and charisma of a single dynamic leader. The strength of these teams is found in their blending of leaders who have complementary gifts and skills, their mutual passion for the same vision, a desire to give the credit to God rather than seek it for themselves and the ability to work within the parameters set for their team by the senior pastor, who typically serves as a "super leader" overseeing all leadership activity within the ministry.

These senior pastors deserve a lot of credit for controlling their egos long enough to give resources and platforms to other quality leaders. In the end, these pastors appear to be much stronger and capable than they are simply because of their willingness to turn loose the cumulative leadership capacity embodied within the congregation. En route to doing so, these pastors affirm and facilitate the leaders that form the core teams; that endorsement and continual support allow the teams to prosper.

The genius of this style of leadership is in the collaborative nature of the leader-follower relationship. Essentially, the pastor becomes a visionary team-builder, more of a player-coach than the owner of a sports franchise. Just like a player-coach, he must maintain the balance of positional authority and personal leadership. He is given the authority to lead as long as he gets results. He calls many plays strategically but he must also fulfill his role as a player on whom others depend. Unlike a monarchy, he does not have the right to rule by reason of birth; he earns respect, authority and responsibility through his performance. (Some scholars assert that black Baptist churches of the United States were influenced by African tribal traditions whereby once a leader was enthroned, he was able to rule with great authority but that freedom to wield power was severely reduced when a series of unwise decisions shattered the confidence of the tribe.)[5]

In some ways, this team-orientation may be one of the greatest legacies of black leadership: the desire to form coalitions of like-minded people who will use their gifts to labor side by side and foster positive outcomes, without regard to personal acclaim. In spite of living in an environment in which image and reputation are primary, numerous black leaders have toiled in anonymity, working behind the scenes to introduce serious change in the families, neighborhoods, communities or regions in which they minister. Black pastors generally feel at ease with the idea of being the captain of a team rather than having to be the omnipotent and omniscient ruler of a nation. The respect they get from their congregants and the unity of focus that results compensate for any absence of public applause received. That, in fact, is one of many indicators that these are pastors involved in ministry for the right reasons.

4. Refusal to Micromanage the Ministry

One of the most often heard complaints about pastors is their tendency to micromanage the ministry. This penchant for control, however, is absent in effective black churches. There are several reasons for this. One reason is that genuine leaders realize that such meddling only restrains the church from making progress. Another is the fact that most pastors are either directing leaders (meaning they are big-picture, visionary types who have limited interest in the details) or team-building leaders (indicating their interest is in people, not process). Yet another reason is the different type of relationship that black pastors have with their congregants. Geared to developing a truly interdependent work relationship, pastors are generally thrilled to leave the administrative dimension to people who are gifted in the area and whose passion for systems and details frees the pastor to do the challenging and exciting ministry tasks that he does best.

There may be some historical reasons for the tendency to avoid micromanaging, too. Many of the current black church leadership structures have their roots in the rural, southern, post-Civil War environment in which the black church flourished. Most rural communities could not afford a full-time pastor, resulting in the recruitment of part-time leaders. Thus, while the hired pastor did the preaching and other ceremonial duties, the board of deacons ran the day-to-day affairs of the church.

More often than not, the chairman of the deacons became a de facto pastor. The head deacon and the pastor had to forge a healthy working relationship since the unity between these leaders would determine the stability and potential of their church.[6] As modernization redefined society and ministry, the tendency of lay leaders to carry out many of the administrative and other nonessential ministry functions was retained. This arrangement has made the "priesthood of all believers" more than just a quaint Bible phrase. It has assisted the laity in enjoying the freedom to minister while permitting the pastor to focus on clarifying, communicating, protecting and advancing the primary vision for the ministry.

5. Investment in Developing Effective Followers

God creates some to lead and some to follow but all of us must refine whichever capacity has been entrusted to us. One of the secrets of effective pastoring is knowing how to develop people into good followers. More than four out of every five congregants have not been called by God to serve in a leadership capacity but those who are called to follow the leader need to know how to do so effectively. Many pastors assume that if they lead, people will follow. They will—but they'll probably do so poorly. Great followers are worth their weight in gold—and nearly as rare.

Effective black pastors have a keen sense of legacy: the people whose lives their ministry has touched. But to leave behind a cadre of great followers consumes a substantial parcel of resources. Our observation is that growing great followers takes the five Ts:

- **Time**—There are no shortcuts; plan on allocating many hours each week to raising up world-class followers.
- **Training**—Encouragement, instruction, feedback and supervised participation are part of the process.
- **Tracks**—Routines and practices that become part of the continuity make following possible and efficient.
- **Truth**—Honest feedback and godly wisdom are dispensed by someone who loves them and the Master whom they serve.
- **Trust**—Mutual respect and honor enable the relationship to grow constantly.

Eliminating or muting any of these effectively shortchanges the follower and limits his or her ability to add value through contributing to the congregation as a follower.

What can leaders do to grow terrific followers? According to the examples we witnessed, the first step is to engage the follower with the vision and values of the ministry. Until the individual is sold out to those perspectives, he or she is simply playing a game and consuming resources. Further, followers must know themselves well enough to identify their gifts and skills and to seek ways of using those capacities for the advancement of the vision. Followers must also hold themselves to a high standard of performance. With church leaders motivating them to serve and mentoring them to excellence, followers can make ministry fun, productive and transforming.

When a leader is smart enough to realize that he is only as good as his followers enable him to be, then he has the motivation he needs to invest ample resources in those followers. They are not just faceless units that add girth to the ministry; they are the lifeblood of the ministry and must be handled appropriately. Developing a culture of growth and respect for everyone brings about a ministry that is invulnerable because it has the two indispensable ingredients for effectiveness: vision-driven servant-leaders and vision-driven servant-followers.

6. Impact Through Collaboration

Once again, the history of Christian ministry in America explains one of the distinctive patterns seen in the black church today. More than a century ago, before automobiles and telephones reoriented the ways and places in which we live, many churches were led by pastors who oversaw multiple congregations. To get to those groups, preachers had to ride by horseback from one location to another. These preachers, known as circuit riders, were obviously limited in terms of how much time and attention they could devote to administrative details, organizational structure, person-to-person communications, meetings and so forth.

Black pastors often converted this limitation into strength by developing social and spiritual connections among the various churches they led. Though separated by physical distance, these disparate congregations began to see the value of collaboration in ministry and occasionally joined together for larger works of social justice and faith building. That sense of oneness despite geographic isolation served the civil rights movement well in the latter half of the twentieth century.

That same spirit of partnership has enabled a relatively small and underfinanced population—blacks—to make huge gains through cooperative, church-based efforts. The strength of the black church network is such that presidential candidates these days continue to court leading pastors in the hope of penetrating those groups and receiving endorsements, funding, volunteers and, of course, votes. The chances are high that if such value was not placed upon united ministry, black churches would be ignored by political candidates.

Black pastors rely upon such coalitions in order to see tangible progress. This strategy, however, has meant subjugating personal ego for the benefit of the people, reorienting schedules to accommodate the time-consuming process of building and maintaining relationships with partner churches, surrendering total control of their ministry agenda, accepting some compromise in desired positions in order to have the power of the larger group operating on their behalf and having to invest precious ministry dollars in activities that may not be managed to their liking. There is, in other words, a price to pay for working collaboratively but the impetus is their zeal to see personal and social transformation occur. Many black pastors reminded us that the price for *not* serving in tandem with their spiritual brothers and sisters in other churches is more difficult to swallow in the long run.

7. The Significance of Longevity
One of the important ministry lessons we have learned through our research is that a leader needs longevity and continuity to

introduce significant and lasting change. We have estimated that most pastors experience their greatest impact on and through a congregation from the fifth through the fourteenth year of their leadership in their church. The first several years are invested in developing relationships and trust, selling the vision, structuring for efficacy, evaluating current processes and future opportunities, and establishing a foundation for momentum.

Effective black pastors have been at their churches longer than the norm. In fact, the typical white pastor leaves the church he is serving before the start of his fifth year; the typical black pastor serves nearly twice as long. This reflects not only the patience of the black community in bringing about change but also the higher levels of satisfaction with the efforts of their pastor. Naturally, the more the congregation is on board with the vision and the work of the pastor, the more likely he is to stay at the church and seek to finish what God has started through him.

8. Always Leading, Always Growing

The twenty-first century will continue to birth rapid innovations and an explosion of information. Futurists tell us that the amount of knowledge we have access to will actually double several times in our lifetime. In light of this glut of information, doctors, lawyers and other professionals have developed many continuing education forums and classes just to keep up. The clergy must also challenge themselves to keep up in terms of ongoing biblical, social and psychological study.

In general, the black clergy members, have taken upon themselves the challenge to stay relevant. According to our surveys, they feel their ministry career has been fulfilling and beneficial. Nine out of 10 strongly agree that their pastoral ministry has deepened their relationship with Christ. Nine out of 10 contend that pastoring their current church has increased their passion for ministry. Half allude to their desire to have a broad impact on the world by noting that their present position has afforded them "significant influence" on public and social policy.

In terms of formal education, black pastors outstrip their congregations significantly, while modeling the concept of life-long learning. Conversations with black pastors suggest that their means of learning are often different from those of their white counterparts: They are not as likely to read a lot of books. Black culture and tradition have been passed on largely through oral communication and the pastoral world is no different. Much of the growth that happens is traceable to personal inter-action among pastors through breakfast meetings, conferences, denominational forums and other face-to-face gatherings.

In current parlance, of course, this is known as "viral com-munication"—the passage of wisdom and ideas through nonfor-mal means. This is one reason why black churches often seem to jump on issues and opportunities more rapidly than other organizations. With aggressive, risk-taking leaders at the helm who are sensitive to changing conditions, black churches have been able to exploit advantages in timing that would not have been available had they waited for books, journals, classes and other highly structured forms of information conveyance to introduce such insights.

9. Building the Adaptable Model

In many nations of the world there are congregations reaching sizes of 20,000 members or more. Churches that large typically have mastered many leadership principles and skills that allow them the capacity to minister effectively to the masses without losing their impact on individual lives.

The best international models are both flexible and scalable.

Scalability implies a firm foundation that allows the organization to grow dramatically in size without having to change its foundational structure and procedures. Most American churches would not pass the flexibility or scalability tests—largely because they have not freed and empowered gifted leaders to lead. Our examination of effective black churches found that many of them are poised to grow unusually large—and dozens of them have. (As we stated earlier, the number of black churches that are home to 15,000 or more congregants is perhaps one of the best-kept secrets in the ministry world. While Willow Creek or Saddleback is consistently touted by the mass media as the largest church in America, there are numerous black churches of equal or greater size.)

The flexibility and growth potential are more common in black churches because of the clergy-laity partnership and the time-honored tradition of experimentation with new approaches to ministry. While all churches, black or otherwise, have their struggles with the "sacred cows" of ministry—traditions that everyone has become comfortable with even though they may hinder the health and advancement of the ministry—the philosophical willingness to give the senior leader more latitude and the congregational emphasis on product rather than process have enabled the effective churches to build for a future that is different from the past and present.

Among the practices and perspectives that contribute to this preparation for growth are the consistency of senior pastors who have prioritized their effort to the extent that they know which battles to fight and which ones are mere distractions from what matters; the joy of delegation; the regularity of training people for maximum ministry impact in relation to their gifts, passion and willingness to serve; and sensitivity to the superb instincts of the leaders who are invested in the ministry.

A Leader's Joy and Grind

No organization will go beyond the place where its leader is able to take it. If the black church in America has not made as much headway as some think it should have, the responsibility largely rests on the shoulders of black pastors. But the undeniable effect of the black church in this country also points to the existence of pastors who have used their gift of leadership appropriately.

No organization will go beyond the place where its leader is able to take it.

As Scripture forewarns, no victory comes without a price (see Luke 14:25-33). This truth is every bit as evident in ministry as in any other dimension of life. One area in which even the most effective black pastors admit that the ravages of spiritual warfare are most keenly felt is in their family life. (About half of the black pastors surveyed admitted that pastoring has been tougher than expected and a similar proportion noted that leading churches has taken a significant toll on their family.) Many other black pastors echo the despair of their white, Hispanic, Asian and Native American peers who contend that pastoring is a lonely job—as great leadership always is. But a driving force in these ministries is the fact that African-Americans remain attuned to the fact that there is more to life than meets the eye: There is an eternity in heaven that awaits those who love, obey and serve the Lord.

CHAPTER 3

TRAINED MINDS, TRANSFORMED LIVES

The more I converse with this people, the more I am amazed. . . .
It is plain, God begins His work at the heart; then "the inspiration
of the highest giveth understanding."

—JOHN WESLEY

Over the past decade, it has become evident that there are two types of disciple-making churches in America today. One type seeks to develop people who become a reflection of the dictionary definition of "disciple": those who are "a pupil or an adherent of another—a follower."[1] Consequently, we could say that most people are disciples of the president (whomever it may be at any given moment) or their boss at work. In fact, by using that definition most Americans could be described as followers of Jesus. After all, most people know a lot about Him, most Americans consider themselves to be Christians, a large majority are generally in favor of His perspectives, and almost everyone regularly exhibits behavior influenced by His teachings. In that sense, the Church in the United States has done a good job of making disciples.

And yet, few people would forcefully argue that America is a land of true disciples of Jesus. The reason is that being a true disciple takes more than intellectual knowledge and emotional assent to a way of life. It demands the total embracing of and immersion in the way of life espoused by the leader.

Jesus did not die on the cross simply so that people would know about Him and then pick and choose the principles they like from the full slate of principles and practices He embodied. He died so that all people might rethink the purpose and nature of their lives and choose to live for the love and sake of God the

Jesus did not die on the cross simply so that people would know about Him and then pick and choose the principles they like from the full slate of principles and practices He embodied.

Father. A more circumspect consideration of Jesus' teachings shows that His goal was not simply to gain followers but to attract *zealots*. Throughout His earthly ministry He admonished His followers to pick up the pace and sell out to His prescribed ways of thinking and being. In like manner, Scripture exhorts the Church to cultivate not mere followers but intense zealots—that is, people who are driven to become Christlike in every aspect of their lives. In this regard, the American Church—black, white or otherwise—has not fulfilled its mandate.

As we studied high-impact African-American churches, it became obvious that there is something very different about the way in which they approach discipleship. These churches see themselves as being at war with modern and postmodern culture. Rather than accepting moral and spiritual decay as the natural and unavoidable state of our society in which the role of a church is to apply a bandage over a gaping wound, these churches see themselves as miracle workers intent upon bringing complete healing and restoration to a desperately ill and dying people. Their methods and attitudes are unlike those at most churches, even those of most black churches. These are churches that have built their ministry of creating zealots for Christ on a unique heritage.

SLAVE OR FREE?

Despite the hostile culture that surrounded it, the black church in colonial America nurtured blacks to adopt an entirely new perspective on life based upon an understanding of the kingdom of God. While the human kingdom that shaped the nation demonstrated wanton disregard for the lives of the lowly, God's kingdom elevated the undesirables to a place of value and honor. By presenting the Bible as a document of practical wisdom rather than one of theological doublespeak, black ministers led their people on a journey designed to distinguish their differences from the dominant culture rather than one bent on accommodating it.

Among the many black ministers who faithfully served God and His people during the early years of the United States, Daniel Payne is an example of a leader who helped people experience deeper meaning in life. Payne's battle against ignorance and stereotypes was not solely directed at changing the thinking of whites. He knew that blacks had to be convinced they could overcome their own ignorance, so he developed a strategy to attack black hopelessness and self-doubt.

Born in South Carolina in 1811, Payne's lineage was racially mixed—black, white and Native American. As a free man, he was not subjected to the nonexistent or poor education that abounded in the slave community during that era. Payne became a self-styled man of letters, learning French, Greek and Latin. Despite his intellectual achievements, the pigment of his skin forced him to identify with the plight of the average black man.[2]

After completing his early education at the age of 17, Payne had the vision and confidence to establish his own school. Acknowledging that blacks lagged behind the educational progress of whites by a huge margin, Payne conceived a two-pronged strategy. First, he taught black children the basics during the day, providing a quality education for children who would normally have been left behind without a second thought. Second, he devoted his evenings to teaching black adults after their long, tiring hours of manual labor. Payne epitomized a purpose-driven approach to maturing the believers under his care. He overcame the barriers of limited finances and persecution to leave a lasting legacy.

Payne is best known as the sixth bishop of the African Methodist Episcopal (AME) Church and as the denomination's preeminent historian. He left an indelible mark on the AME Church by goading them into establishing universities for black students and challenging their ministers to provide strong biblical teaching. In 1856, Bishop Payne founded Wilberforce University with the intention of integrating faith and practical career training for African-Americans. As the first president of the university, Payne introduced the concept of ensuring that even those who were trained for a secular career would have the benefit of practical theology as the basis of all they did in life. While his nation was fighting a bloody civil war, Payne was fighting to evangelize and disciple an entire race.

For Payne, faith and education were interconnected. He felt

that a person's faith could raise him or her above the problems of the day and give that person courage to face the world. Simultaneously, practical skills were needed to help an individual excel in the world's economic structures. This dual educational approach made the AME denomination culturally relevant in ways that the black church had not previously considered. Payne's vision and efforts helped the Church turn the cultural tide in America.

What if churches discipled their brightest and best young people in the Scriptures and then sent them into the culture's hot spots of influence?

Imagine Payne's approach in our modern era. What if churches discipled their brightest and best young people in the Scriptures and then sent them into the culture's hot spots of influence—music, visual arts, sports, public policy and education? What would the culture look like if more of our role models and influencers approached their craft from a biblical worldview?

Fortunately, there are hundreds of ministers with Daniel Payne's passion and practicality leading African-American churches today. In an era when ministers are tempted to soften their messages and water down content in order to attract people and minimize conflict, many black churches are laying strong scriptural foundations in the lives of their people. With the Bible as their foremost textbook, these ministers are equipping their members to attain the highest levels of both spiritual and secular success.

The Current Situation

The black population, like other ethnic groups, struggles with the content and practice of its faith. Regardless of a person's color, the American culture relentlessly distracts people from the matters of God. Striving to help people stay focused on Him and His principles is an uphill battle, even for the best of ministries. Certainly what makes the effective black churches stand out is their ability to get people on the right path, both theologically and behaviorally.

Such focus is badly needed. Our most recent studies show that the involvement of black adults in faith activities generally exceeds that of whites and Hispanics, but we must also remember that outperforming other racial groups is not the mark of success. God has established a standard that is difficult to reach but challenges all people equally, regardless of their ethnic background.

If the goal of the African-American church is to help transform blacks into spiritual zealots, then we can see that progress has been made but that there is plenty of room for further growth. Gauging what takes place in a typical week, the following facts pertain to blacks and their religious practices:

- Slightly more than half (56 percent) read the Bible at times other than when they are at church. (The comparable figure for whites is 37 percent; for Hispanics, 35 percent.)
- Not quite half (47 percent) attend church services. (The comparable figure for whites is 42 percent; for Hispanics, 45 percent.)
- More than 9 out of 10 (92 percent) pray to God. (The comparable figure for whites is 78 percent; for Hispanics, 84 percent.)

- Nearly 3 out of 10 (28 percent) attend Sunday School. (The comparable figure for whites is 19 percent; for Hispanics, 23 percent.)
- Three out of 10 blacks (30 percent) participate in a small group. (The comparable figure for both whites and Hispanics is 18 percent.)
- One out of every 7 blacks (14 percent) fasts for religious purposes in a typical week. (The comparable figure for whites is 6 percent; for Hispanics, 10 percent.)[3]

These statistics indicate that blacks are generally more involved in religious activities than are adults from other ethnic backgrounds. One of our tracking measures is what we label "active faith"—that is, people who attend church, read the Bible and pray during a given week. Blacks top the list in this regard, with more than one out of every three (36 percent) meeting the criteria. That is about one-third higher than the proportion of whites (25 percent) or Hispanics (24 percent) who have an active faith.

Our research concerning people's beliefs is somewhat less encouraging. We find very little indecision on the part of adults and even teenagers regarding their spiritual beliefs; in other words, people know what they believe and indicate little inclination to alter those perspectives. But an examination of those beliefs leads us to conclude we might be better off if people's minds were more open to change. If we examine just a few of the core beliefs that help to define a person's worldview and his or her understanding of Christianity, we find that millions of people, including blacks, mean well but are offtrack. For instance, our national studies in 2003 revealed the following:

- Only 22 percent of black adults strongly disagree that Satan is just a symbol of evil but does not exist.

- Just 30 percent of black adults strongly disagree that a good person cannot earn his or her way into heaven because of his or her laudable works.
- Not even half of black adults (48 percent) strongly disagree that Jesus committed sins while He was on Earth.
- One out of every four blacks (23 percent) has some notion of God other than the biblical description of His nature and character—loving, pure, omniscient, omnipotent, the creator of the universe, the reigning ruler of all things.
- Barely more than one out of every four (27 percent) believe that absolute moral truth exists.
- Less than half believe that they have a responsibility to share their spiritual convictions about Christ and salvation with other people.

While we may be excited to learn that a huge majority of blacks (85 percent) contend that their religious faith is very important in their lives and that most black adults (60 percent) are convinced that the Bible is accurate in all of its teachings, there are obviously some loose connections related to the substance of their faith. (For the sake of cultural context, it might also be pointed out that the statistics for each of these measures pertaining to the white population are even less affirming.)

Formation Distinctives

As in the white ministry world, the churches that are facilitating remarkable spiritual growth among blacks base their ministry efforts upon a different set of perspectives and practices. Across the board, we find that the most impactful churches incorporate most, if not all, of seven specific approaches to forming zealots. Let's delve into the substance of the approaches that work most effectively.

1. Leadership for Discipleship

Postmodern America is ripe for dramatic spiritual transformation but no serious change will occur unless courageous leaders redefine reality, develop the means to change and give people irresistible reasons for participating in the reengineering of their lives. The experience of effective black churches indicates that churches need not throw up their hands in despair and cave in to the prevailing culture. Instead, we must simply reach out to people in a slightly different manner and guide them along a different path of development.

A leader's paradigm can either lift people higher or become a lid that impedes their growth. For instance, if a pastor believes that his congregation lacks the desire or aptitude to learn, he is not likely to invest the time and energy required to train his people. But if that same pastor sees the shortcomings of his congregation as a challenge that must be understood and overcome, he will then convert the information about weaknesses into life-changing strategies for growth.

A congregation cannot go where its leaders refuse to take it. Conversely, if a leader is enthusiastic and adamant about growth, then the congregation will likely follow. As with any aspect of life change, someone must motivate the individuals involved to believe that growth is possible, to desire growth and to follow determinedly a designated path to facilitate that growth.

The absence of courageous and strategic leadership is an insurmountable spiritual handicap for many churches. The low expectations of leaders often become self-fulfilling prophecies, limiting the spiritual destiny of their followers.

Leaders should never be obstacles to people's growth. Great

pastors set the bar high; they refuse to believe that their people can or should be anything less than what God made them to be. In high-impact churches the leaders make a compelling argument for the necessity of personal spiritual maturity—and for paying the price to reach that state of being. Our observation is that some members of the congregation run from the challenge and may leave but most people have the self-confidence and the innate desire to cause them to line up behind truth-speaking, truth-seeking leaders.

Such courage among leaders has been evident in black churches for many decades. During the times of slavery, black ministers spoke out against cruelty and injustice, founding their critiques upon the worth of every created being, the morality of equality and other arguments that reflected a biblical worldview. Those ministers often suffered along with the people whose hopes and dreams they defended—and, in so doing, established an unforgettable model of what a life of spiritual zealotry looks like.

Courageous leadership of the discipling process means that the leader models exactly what is being demanded of the followers; a substantial treasury of resources will be invested in the developmental process; everyone will be invited—and expected—to participate or will suffer tangible and identifiable consequences, the leader will maintain constant surveillance on the growth curves of measurable outcomes; and the leader's communications with the congregation will invariably incorporate the centrality of personal and corporate spiritual growth as a centerpiece of the ministry.

2. A Clear Discipleship Philosophy

As we also discovered in our explorations of effective white churches, high-impact African-American congregations base their discipleship efforts on a clear philosophy of how spiritual growth works and what it takes for a church to facilitate such outcomes. Our surveys show that virtually every pastor and every church leader say that they want people to grow spiritually. Effective churches go beyond simply *desiring* growth and development in the lives of their people. Instead, they create a clear-cut, measurable training strategy for accomplishing the goal. The leaders of these churches recognize that faith development should affect belief systems, values, character and behavior. These things only line up when biblical principles have been communicated and demonstrated by the church leadership team.

The philosophy usually includes these critical elements:

- A succinct and clear description of the relevant subjects—discipleship, biblical literacy, spiritual maturity, accountability and so forth.
- A well-defined assignment of responsibilities within the maturation process. (Teachers have specified responsibilities, as do students and the church; these responsibilities are laid out as the basis for structures, policies and assignments.)
- A description of effectiveness in discipleship but also identify specific ways of measuring progress toward individual maturity and ministry impact.

3. Blending Evangelism and Discipleship

A Barna Research survey conducted several years ago found that more than 9 out of every 10 Protestant churches contend that they are "committed to the Great Commission." However, our explorations of church practices since that time have also revealed that most churches interpret Matthew 28:19-20 to be about evangelism. A realistic examination of the text indicates that Jesus' parting exhortation is about both evangelism *and* discipleship. Evangelism without discipleship leaves new converts spiritually immature and vulnerable; discipleship without evangelism results in isolated and ineffectual training for its own sake.

Effective churches realize that successful ministry cannot be judged by attendance figures, size of budget, number of programs offered or even the awareness of reputation of a church. Success is based on life transformation. That transformation begins with a person's inviting Jesus Christ to be his or her Lord and Savior. The transformation is then facilitated by maturing in knowledge, wisdom, obedience, service, love, character and worship—tangible expressions of genuine faith and a true relationship with God. It is the discipleship enterprise that facilitates such development.

As one pastor explained the process, nonbelievers generally come to faith in Christ through the encouragement and guidance of a mature disciple. In turn, that new believer demonstrates his or her rebirth as a citizen of the Kingdom by relentlessly pursuing the heart and mind of God. That commitment to being like Christ is partially exemplified by his or her dedication to leading other nonbelievers into the Kingdom and helping them in their subsequent spiritual formation.

4. Providing Practical Theology

One of the laity's most consistent criticisms of the Church is that the teaching and preaching are not pertinent to their lives. Effective churches—especially those in the black community— avoid this critique by presenting the Bible's timeless theological principles as practical theology; that is, truth that is understandable and applicable to everyday life. Dale Andrews described the approach of the best black churches as one that accepts the challenge to make theology relevant to the common man and the common condition.

> We simply do not identify . . . with many of the complex, esoteric, and impersonal theological concepts or doctrines held up before us. Indeed, while theologians go to extraordinary lengths to re-conceptualize and articulate the life of faith, the actual struggle to find theology practical wrestles with the meaning of life and the daily experiences of living.[4]

High-impact black churches do a superb job of elevating the authority of Scripture while bringing down-to-earth messages that touch the heart. Historically, black church leaders have empowered their members with tools of true faith despite the hardship of their immediate circumstances. James Deotis Roberts noted that black churches addressed the most difficult and enduring problems that black people faced:

> Instead of hatred and revenge, [their] Christian faith enabled [them] to transmute suffering into many victories in [their] own lives and in the lives of other blacks and whites.[5]

Theology therefore has become more than just intellectualized pulpit content; it is the foundation for responding to the crises and hardships that have characterized the black experience in this country.

One of the secrets of these churches is their ability to make theology tenable by offering it in the context of the personal

benefits it delivers to the end user. Much like professional salesmen extolling the benefits of a particular product, so many
polished black leaders teach the benefits of the gospel with bold-
ness and clarity. Rather than take the simplistic and ultimately
self-defeating approach of simply bashing the competition,
these pastors and teachers help congregants grasp the principles
and their personal applications. In the course of doing so, they
confront the tough theological and lifestyle issues that arise, and
they also refute the claims of cults by unmasking the foundational claims of these groups without calling them by name. The
ultimate end, however, is quite simple: to equip each believer
with sufficient understanding of the Bible to develop a worldview that will produce a Christlike life.

Making theology practical requires teachers who are able to
think through the material they wish to communicate and
answer the bottom-line question: So what? Black churches, in
particular, seem to dislike theology transmitted for its own sake;
the prevailing perspective seems to be "make it real." We discovered that adults and young people in black churches give high
marks to their teachers—in Sunday School, study groups and
other classroom settings—because the church recruits teachers
carefully and prepares them for success.

How do these churches select their teachers? Naturally, the
desire to teach and adequate Bible knowledge are prerequisites.
Perhaps the more important qualification is the desire to move
students beyond information and inspiration to *life integration*.
The teaching candidate is encouraged to help students develop a
Christian worldview or at least to approach the material to be
covered from such a holistic theological point of view. Not surprisingly, Jesus Himself rejected the popular Greek model of
instruction in favor of a principle-based approach that invariably
connected those principles to real-life issues. He gave His disci-

ples exercises, and He evaluated and critiqued their efforts. Like Jesus, teachers in effective churches go beyond mere head knowledge—they teach information to facilitate better life choices.

To their credit, the great churches do not simply identify mature believers, those with the gift of teaching, and turn them loose on students. These ministries invest in their teachers, giving them instruction in methods and content. We learned that more often than not, consultants or master teachers are brought in from the outside to lift the skill level of the church's instructors—hands-on training is not left up to the pastor or church staff. The training is targeted to the level and needs of the individual teachers as much as possible—there is little in the way of generic training that is supposed to meet the needs of all teachers. These churches also refuse to require their teachers to devote themselves to completing administrative trivia or attending unnecessary "touch base" meetings. Protecting the time and energy of teachers is one way these churches show their respect for the gift their teachers bring.

5. Offering Many Means of Growing

One of the recent trends in Christian education has been the diversification of means by which people absorb spiritual information and experiences. Whereas the old regimen was Sunday School, Sunday worship, Sunday-night services and Wednesday-evening services, mostly featuring the teaching of the senior pastor, people's schedules and expectations are radically different these days. Even though black families spend more time in church on Sunday than do folks from any other ethnic background, the name of the game is still options. People want to choose from a menu that allows them to tailor a spiritual agenda that meets their multifaceted needs.

While it is a struggle for small churches to do so, the most effective churches offer people a variety of alternatives for spiritual growth. The usual offerings—the worship service and Sunday School—are always present. In addition, special options are offered, such as small groups, elective classes, special events, off-premises seminars and conferences, individual mentoring, workplace meetings, service clubs, online courses, satellite teaching programs and more. Even the Christian media—especially radio—have been integrated into the discipleship prescription of many churches, with the blessing of the church leaders. Indeed, to win people's time and commitment these days, the agenda of possibilities generally reflects options that are creative, flexible and of high quality.

Keep in mind that offering various options is not the same as empowering and equipping genuine zealots. Developing and executing a healthy discipleship model demand some formidable and carefully evaluated goals. Methods must transcend the traditional lecture format. In a world in which video cell phones, digital photography, the Internet and instantaneous global communications are the norm, getting people to devote themselves to faith development demands new strategies and techniques.

Frankly, one of the secrets of success in these congregations is that they joyfully celebrate the success of their people. Growth is often uncomfortable, and it certainly consumes personal resources (time, energy, money). To encourage people's continued involvement and to motivate others to join in the journey, effective churches tend to call attention to those who meet specified, predetermined growth goals. This process of rewarding those who grow reinforces the practical value of spiritual development for all who are associated with the ministry while giving a special emotional and psychological boost to the believers who performed well.

6. Faith Without Works Is Dead

To the greatest extent of any of the ethnic churches we have studied, black churches emphasize the significance of blending faith and works. There is no fine line to walk. These churches are crystal clear that works do not produce salvation but they are

> *Life-changing black churches tailor spiritual-development materials to the unique needs of their people.*

similarly dogmatic about the weakness of faith that is not demonstrated through Spirit-led acts of service.

It is truly heartwarming to witness the dedication that these churches have in assisting their people in *being* the Church, rather than merely coming to a church. Just as we would contend that a great ballplayer is one who plays the game at the highest level rather than someone who can report what happened in a game, so do we assert that a great church is one in which its people serve others without complaint or resentment. It is the desire and willingness to serve those in need, without hesitation, which show a person's understanding of the gift of his or her salvation.

7. Spiritual Substance

Increasingly, it appears that life-changing black churches tailor spiritual-development materials to the unique needs of their people. Depending on what is available and what is needed, they often cut and paste existing materials with resources they create to satisfy their unique needs. We need to recognize that this is possible because these churches know their people well enough to identify and even customize resources to meet those needs.

Princeton professor Cornell West has observed that black theology and biblical teaching have often had a prophetic dimension to them. He believes that black churches focused on critiquing American culture from 1969 to 1977 and then shifted to critiquing capitalism from 1977 to 1982. Most recently, it seems that the emphasis in black ministries has been upon lessons related to blacks in the Bible, as well as prosperity and personal economic improvement. The coming years will undoubtedly bring a transition in the topics of interest but the pattern is clear: Churches remain sensitive to the needs and concerns of their constituency and respond with real-world counsel and Kingdom wisdom.

CHAMP OR CHUMP?

Every successful contemporary church—black, white or multicultural—should be aware of Tom Peters's observation that the pace of change in our society means that any organization can move from "champ to chump" in only five years.[6] American culture is changing so rapidly that a product or service could be celebrated today and entirely ignored in fewer than five years.

This is certainly true for churches as well. In some ways, our teaching and faith training are products that we offer to our constituents. Maintaining cultural relevance is very similar to hitting a moving target. Churches that endure and succeed must master the art of infiltrating their local communities so that they can present timeless truths with freshness.

But let's also take Peters's challenge and turn it around. Churches that currently fall into the "chump" category—i.e., those that are not effectively evangelizing non-Christians, discipling church members and helping people to grow spiritually—can become "champs." They must become convinced that spiritual growth is inextricably linked to biblical understanding and doctrinal clarity. Then these churches must get about the business of creatively and compellingly integrating the Word of God into the lives of their members. Is this a big challenge? You bet. But we serve a God who delights in working through His children to overcome big challenges and beat overwhelming odds.

CHAPTER 4

WORSHIP: ENCOUNTERS WITH THE ALMIGHTY

Worship is to quicken the conscience by the holiness of God, to feed the mind with the truth of God, to purge the imagination by the beauty of God, to open up the heart to the love of God, to devote that will to the purpose of God.

—WILLIAM TEMPLE

Suppose you stopped 10 people on the street and asked, "What's the first thing that pops into your head when you think of black churches?" Most of those folks would respond, "Great music!"

It's true that the African-American church has traditionally featured upbeat, inspirational and stirring music—this tradition continues today. Indeed, it's no secret that black churches have been the training ground for many international recording artists. From Whitney Houston to Aretha Franklin, Al Green to Curtis Mayfield and Patti LaBelle to Toni Braxton, numerous artists have been impacted by the black church's style and expression.

A True Definition of Worship

Most Christians would agree that worship is one of the primary functions and activities of every church—most people would further agree that music is integral to worship. We would do well, then, to determine exactly what we mean when we use the word "worship."

Worship is undeniably a major theme of the Bible. In fact, the significance of worship can be recognized by the fact that it is referred to in three of the first four of the Ten Commandments (see Exodus 20:2-11). These admonitions against false worship and the failure to engage in worship did not tell the Israelites *how* to worship God so much as to exhort them to ensure that they engaged Him—and *only* Him—in worship. By providing the motivation but not the methods related to worship, the Lord left open the door for varied expressions of our hearts to Him, resulting in the widespread styles of worship encountered in churches and denominations around the world today.

From the numerous examples in the Bible of people worshiping God, we deduce that the overriding impetus to worship is the individual's need to relate to God—and His passionate desire for us to relate to Him in an appropriate manner. Worshipers in the Scriptures interact with God as an expression of love, allegiance and awe for their creator. Fundamentally, worship is an intimate, individual act that creates an exchange between God and a person.

Judson Cornwall, a noted writer on the subject of worship, offers the following insight into the practice of connecting with God:

> The English word *worship* comes from the old English word *weordhscipe,* which was later shortened to *worthship.*

It is concerned with the worthiness, dignity, or merit of a person or, as in the case of idolatry, a thing. In the English court it is still used as a noun in referring to a dignitary as "his worship." Worship, in the verb form, means the paying of homage or respect, and in the religious world the term is used for the reverent devotion, service, or honor, whether public or individual paid to God.[1]

Despite the availability of such helpful definitions, awareness of the traditions that relate to the practice of honoring and connecting with God in worship, attendance at numerous worship events and exposure to extensive teaching and writing on the subject of worship, most Americans do not really grasp its true meaning. When asked to define "worship," the great majority of American worshipers—black, white, Hispanic, Asian or Native American—were unable to provide a reasonable explanation. Amazingly, our surveys requesting a specific definition of "worship" found that the most common reply is "I don't know." Other common descriptions of what worship is—such as attending church, becoming a church member or even believing that God exists—reflect the paucity of understanding resident within the churchgoing community.[2]

The local church still has the biblical command to help people focus on God and interact with Him. Encouraging people to experience God's presence, individually or corporately, is not an easy task. By studying high-impact churches, we discovered that church leaders must be intentional and deliberate if meaningful worship is to be experienced.

Given the superficial responses of the meaning of "worship," it is not surprising that most churchgoers say that they rarely experience God in their worship services. African-Americans, however, are more likely to say that they have meaningful encounters with God than are people from other ethnic groups. This does not mean that all black churches are doing it right but the statistics reflect a striking difference: 53 percent of black church attenders stated that they frequently experienced the presence of God compared to less than two-fifths among the nonblack churchgoing crowd. Among those who regularly experience God's presence during church worship events, those who have this experience "always" outnumber those who "usually" have it by better than a two-to-one margin (37 percent versus 16 percent).[3]

Our surveys requesting a specific definition of "worship" found that the most common reply is "I don't know."

Identifying the Source

The musical genre now called gospel music has not always been as refined as it is today. Gospel music has gone through many iterations en route to its current prominence. Most of the uniquely American forms of music—jazz, blues, soul music and gospel—emerged from African slaves. Even the black spirituals, which many believe to be the parent of original black music, have evolved because of the continuous innovations by black musicians.

Imagine the early black slave community singing about its homeland—or converted slaves worshiping God with all their hearts. In today's high-tech, fast-paced, sophisticated culture it is hard to envision the style, language or cultural dynamics of their music. Yet the American melting pot helped create a new expression that we now call African-American music. Much of the sound that has become so familiar and appealing to millions of Americans arose directly from the spiritual leanings of the African slaves who landed on colonial shores.

So where did black worship music come from? Thomas Higginson, a white abolitionist who commanded the first freed-slave regiment to fight against the Confederacy, described and documented spirituals a few years after the Civil War. Due to his service with black troops, he became quite a student of African-American Christian music. Higginson observed that some slave songs had coded protest messages embedded in them. In fact, in the beginning of the Civil War, blacks jailed in Georgetown, South Carolina, sang a secret message to each other. They encouraged one another with a familiar chorus that usually declared, "We'll soon be free." Instead of singing those inflammatory words, they sang to one another, "The Lord will call us home." Everyone knew that the real message was about freedom, yet with the wink of the eye and the nod of the head, they sang about the Lord's calling them home.[4]

We see this type of code singing in the days of Frederick Douglass, the runaway slave who became an educator and a powerful voice for abolition. He and his fellow slaves sang, "O Canaan, sweet Canaan, I am bound for the land of Canaan," and "Run to Jesus, shun the danger, I don't expect to stay much longer here." They were singing not only about going to heaven someday but also about reaching the North. Singing "Steal Away to Jesus" was as likely to be an announcement for a secret worship service as a song about salvation.[5]

Aside from using music to convey information, the spirituals, or sorrow songs, were primarily sacred songs that expressed worship to God or spiritual encouragement. Thomas Higginson wrote:

> Often in the starlit evening I returned from some lonely ride by the swift river, or on the clover-haunted barrens, and, entering the camp, have silently approached some glimmering fire, round which the dusty figures moved in the rhythmical barbaric dance the Negroes call a "shout."[6]

Where had the traditions that Higginson observed come from? Were they African or American? Were they inspired by the Holy Spirit or simply by humankind's love of song? Were they from the transcendent culture of the kingdom of heaven or from the sultry shores of West Africa?

It seems that the creativity of Nashville's Fisk University Music Department in 1871 gave birth to the African-American spiritual we think of today. The teachers and students wanted to make the rustic, pulsating beat of the African slave spiritual more appealing to the generation they served. What emerged was a harmonious style that appealed to Western Europeans, making the performances more palatable for American and European audiences of all races. Gone were the spontaneity, foot stomping and exuberant joy. These were replaced by control and musical precision quite different from the worship of the Christian slaves and their descendants.

George White organized the original Fisk Jubilee Singers as part of an elaborate fund-raising plan. An 11-person group, comprising predominately former slaves, toured the United States. The original slave songs were literally a blending of two realities: The African heart expressed itself with Christian lyrics.[7]

Indeed, the songs after the Fisk era were much different from the songs originally described by Higginson.

A Brief History of African-American Worship

There has always been a strong emphasis on rhythm in African preaching, singing, moving and dancing. One distinctive of early African worship was the "shout," as mentioned above. Performed by a group of people, this was called "the ring shout of the slaves." No one is sure where the term "shout" comes from. It has been suggested that the word sounds similar to an Islamic word for dancing or movement, while others have posited that the shout was an extension of tribal worship patterns or even of the cultic practices of voodoo.

The intimate nature of these expressions was communicated by a former slave, Robert Anderson, who described what he saw and experienced in slave meetings:

> The colored people . . . have a peculiar music of their own, which is largely a process of rhythm, rather than written music. Their music is largely . . . a sort of rhythmical chant. It had to do largely with religion and the words adapted to their quaint melodies were largely of a religious nature. The stories of the Bible were placed into words that would fit the music already used by the colored people. While singing these songs, the singers and the entire congregation kept time to the music by the swaying of their bodies or by the patting of the foot or hand.[8]

Years after slavery, Bishop Daniel Payne described attending a meeting in 1878:

They formed a ring and with coats off sung, clapped their hands and stamped their feet in a most ridiculous and heathenish way. I requested the pastor to go and to stop their dancing. . . . I told him also that it was a heathenish way to worship and disgraceful to themselves, the race, and the Christian name.[9]

Payne's reproach might sound harsh to us, yet two very different factors motivated Payne to speak with such authority. The first factor was cultural and the second factor was spiritual. From a cultural perspective, he may have been simply helping the former slaves find expressions of worship more culturally compatible with mainstream practices. He may have wanted them to express their faith in a more dignified manner. After all, the former slaves had been on the continent for more than 250 years. It was time for a change.

More important, the bishop's spiritual concern about drawing a line of demarcation between the practices of God's people and the counterfeit world of voodoo was both appropriate and admirable. Recognizing that Israel had lost its place in God's plan because of syncretism (mixing the worship of Jehovah with that of false gods), we realize that every culture must strive to fulfill the first commandment's edict of having "no other gods" (Exod. 20:3; Deut. 5:7). Therefore, purifying the style and content of worship was not a small concern. Fortunately for our nation, the music that has resulted from this progressive work has turned out to be uniquely American and distinctively Christian, born out of the journey of a specific group of people. As black poetess Phyllis Wheatley wrote:

Twas mercy brought me from Pagan land,
Taught my benighted soul to understand
That there's a God, that there's a Savior too[10]

Over the course of many decades, blacks have continued to influence popular music in the United States. Whether it was through hymns, rhythm and blues, jazz or gospel, the impact of the black sound can be traced directly to the group's religious heritage. In fact, the early settlers and colonists would be shocked to see just how mainstream black music has become in America. Even an examination of the faith-related musical genre reveals the undeniable influence of black music. In 2002, gospel music sales surpassed the former leading genre, adult contemporary pop, for the first time. Black gospel music comprised 19 percent of the Christian contemporary music sold in 2002.[11] If not even 13 percent of American citizens are black, the impact of African-Americans on Christian music is significantly greater than their demographic size would suggest. Keep in mind, of course, that measuring the annual sales of black gospel music does not provide a true sense of the full impact of blacks on the worship music of our day. Black artists perform in many other Christian music genres as well.

THE BUILDING BLOCKS OF MEANINGFUL WORSHIP

Our studies among high-impact churches indicate that there are at least four fundamental building blocks for developing consistently fresh and meaningful worship services. These building blocks are the effective use of music, strong leadership by a music director or team, the effective use of biblical teaching or preaching and consistent congregational engagement and response.

Effective Use of Music

Black church services are, on average, nearly twice as long as those in other Protestant churches, running approximately 2 hours in length compared with the 65- to 75-minute average of most other church services. The extended length has relatively little to do with preaching. The typical sermon in a black church is only a couple of minutes longer than the average-length sermon in a white church. The additional time is typically devoted to expanded portions of music, more extensive prayer time and

> *Great worship leaders are not always great musicians.*

the inclusion of testimonials.[12] Many newer black churches, which serve a suburban membership, are beginning to reduce significantly the length of their service times, yet they still adhere to the basic principles that we have garnered in this study.

Because music is the lifeblood of the African-American church, many black churches use multiple choirs and music groups with unique styles to enhance the worship experience. Most high-impact Caucasian churches shy away from "blended" music in worship (i.e., using multiple musical styles in the same worship event) in favor of sticking with a single, dominant musical style.[13]

Our studies have shown that traditional hymns, black gospel, praise and worship choruses and contemporary Christian styles are being used in varying degrees by black churches, with some churches using all four styles. Approximately 60 percent of

African-American churches use four different styles of music, often employing a different style in each service or changing styles in a given service from week to week. For some congregations these styles represent generational preferences, while in other instances they are more reflective of intentional ministry strategy.[14] This musical diversity is not simply an attempt to cater to an underserved segment of the church (i.e., marketing or church growth) but a means of facilitating personal expression. The nonmusical benefits of this approach within worship includes the positioning that suggests the church has made a place for everyone, that the church is a place where creativity is appreciated and promoted and that people are encouraged to participate in developing the church's musical expressions.

Strong Leadership by a Music Director or Team

In order to facilitate an atmosphere and experience of genuine worship in a church, focused leadership is always necessary. Few senior pastors have the musical gifting or available time to facilitate the development of an effective music program. Therefore, someone must direct traffic in the worship services and plan the smooth operation of the music department. Identifying the right person to fill this role is critical. Brenda Aghahowa, in her book *Praising in Black and White: Unity and Diversity in Christian Worship*, makes this insightful observation about the black church:

> It is possible to "have church" without outstanding preaching, but not without good singing. It can fill the vacuum of a poor sermon. "Good singing" is impassioned, intense, emotional, and spiritually powerful. This is due to the conviction about what sermon the soloists and choir are delivering in song.[15]

Although music directors wear several hats and oversee various endeavors, their job description might be distilled down to three elements:

1. Focus people's attention on God.
2. Help people engage in intimate contact with a loving and holy God.
3. Coordinate the musical selections and performances to facilitate people's focus on and their connection with God.

None of the things mentioned in this chapter can be done without a music director who has the gift of leadership along with musical giftedness. In previous research regarding the leading of worship music, we discovered some of the most critical qualities of high-impact worship leaders. Although our research for this book did not replicate that work, the original research incorporated an investigation of black worship leaders as well, enabling us to draw conclusions about what makes someone an effective worship leader.

One of the foundations of great worship leaders relates to the depth and centrality of their faith in Jesus Christ. These are individuals for whom faith is not compartmentalized nor is leading worship simply a job. They are totally in love with Jesus and view leading worship as a means of expressing their personal devotion to Christ in the company of others. Their character is several notches above that of the typical American because their commitment to their faith has allowed the Holy Spirit to alter the habits, preferences, lifestyle patterns and goals that define their lives. These are people for whom the "fruit of the Spirit" (Gal. 5:22-23) becomes a reality, which in turn assists their efforts to bring people into the presence of a holy God.

Great worship leaders are constant students of Scripture, constantly communicating with God through prayer and song; they are individuals who are determined to grow into the maximum men and women of faith that God made them to be.

Surprisingly, we found that great worship leaders are not always great musicians. In fact, being a world-class musician sometimes appears to be a hindrance to becoming someone who

One of the most striking differences is that the preaching at white churches is often analytic, directed at the head, *while preaching in the black church more often aims for both the* head *and the* heart.

is humble, relies upon God for strength and direction and is focused upon helping nonmusical people use music to experience spiritual renewal. Great worship leaders are good musicians but their gifts are in the areas of leadership and shepherding more than musical composition, arranging and performance.

The dedication to worship is evident in their lives. Their leadership of people's worship is not a ministry stepping-stone—it is an opportunity to take people places where they personally have been and to which they want to return. They are passionate about the experience of worship and try to follow God's guidance, delivered through sensitivity to the Holy Spirit, to direct people's hearts toward God. They are effective in this endeavor partially because they are genuine worshipers and thus have a good sense of when the congregation has achieved a worshipful state of being.

The worship leaders we studied had no problem or hesitation

submitting themselves to the authority of the church's leaders. Their primary focus was God, not themselves, so struggles for power and position were not on their radar screen. Their personal integrity allowed them to conduct their ministry within the framework of the mother church's efforts. Their ministry, in other words, was not about themselves but about doing whatever they could to get people connected to God through resonant worship.

Effective Use of Biblical Teaching or Preaching

Scholars who have studied black preaching style often refer to it as a prophetic ministry. The members of the church expect to receive something from God. In a sense, this sets up the preacher to dispense oracles rather than convey information based on his interpretation of Scripture. W. E. B. DuBois, the famous Harvard-educated black scholar of the 1920s, described this prophetic role in secular terms, calling the black preacher "a leader, politician, an orator, a 'boss,' an intriguer, an idealist."[16] James H. Cone, famous for his *Theology of Liberation*, says:

> The sermon therefore is a prophetic oration wherein the preacher "tells it like it is" according to the divine Spirit who speaks through the preacher.[17]

The prophetic nature of black preaching means that people are going to take what has been said to heart. The passion and rhythm of the preaching don't detract from the message. In fact, to the black congregation, the fire may actually verify the minister's conviction, if not the message's divine origin. Regarding the black preacher's role, Hozell C. Francis made this observation:

> Some people have suggested that "prophetic" black preaching is too emotional and even shallow. However,

the context in which the preaching takes place must be considered before any strict conclusions are drawn. . . . The tradition of black preaching developed in a context of dire circumstances. The need to engender a degree of hope in a climate of despair led to a particular kind of preaching.[18]

The importance of the sermon cannot be overlooked. That relatively brief examination of God's principles is the only exposure to Christian teaching that most churchgoing adults in America have in a typical week, rendering the sermon an important element in the faith development process. The preachers in high-impact churches, regardless of the congregation's demographics, typically strive to ensure that congregants are taught how to hear and handle the Word of God, are lovingly but boldly challenged to examine themselves in light of God's principles and are directed toward an attitude and lifestyle that glorifies God.

Black preaching is most often Bible based, delivered in a lecture format and exegetical (i.e., teaching or preaching that isolates and thoroughly explains a particular passage of Scripture). Exegetical preaching often uses the in-depth discussion of a passage to move toward a practical application of that passage. Our research points out that this preaching style is most common in the largest black churches.

Exegetical preaching can create a love for the Word of God. As the preacher explains a particular biblical text, the Word of God becomes accessible to everyone. The only weakness of a scriptural diet made up predominantly of exegetical preaching is that important biblical topics may not be tackled, although we have learned that high-impact churches either consciously approach such subjects in the flow of their exegesis or else they compensate by exposing people to such information through other high-profile ministry efforts. Over the last 20 years there has been an increase in preaching that is topical rather than exegetical. Topical studies are effective at transferring information about a specific subject or giving the listener a comprehensive understanding of the material being discussed. Half of black pastors said they exclusively use an expository approach in their preaching, while another one-third said they use both topical and expository approaches. Just one out of every five pastors said they only engage in topical preaching.[19]

Teaching from black pulpits is often *inductive* rather than *deductive*. This means that people are drawn in with the heart through storytelling, drama and the arts. The emphasis is often on concrete application of the Word of God. The enthusiasm of the presentation fits the learning styles of both the Buster and the Mosaic generations (i.e., people born from 1984-2002).

Regardless of the preaching style adopted, one of the most striking differences between worship in black and white churches is that the preaching at white churches is often analytic, directed at the *head*, while preaching in the black church context more often aims for both the *head* and the *heart*.

Consistent Congregational Engagement and Response

Our recent national surveys have consistently shown that a growing number of people under the age of 40 feel they need a compelling reason to attend worship services. These people are not going to follow traditional expectations unless they are personally convinced that there is personal benefit and meaning to be gained from satisfying such expectations. The credo of many young adults seems to be, "I believe in God but I worship Him in my own way." Highly effective churches often make an intentional effort to dialogue with young adults and help them understand the meaning and importance of worship. Without this kind of personal engagement, many churches lose young adults who don't see the value of corporate worship.

The atmosphere of celebration at high-impact black churches appeals to many young adults who have been raised in a culture that is saturated with entertainment, marketing and hedonism. The upbeat feel of the black worship celebration speaks to the sense of adventure and need for personal experience that move them; the opportunity to establish a divine connection individually fulfills their innate drive to nurture their spiritual essence. High-impact black churches, in particular, connect with many young adults through the animated yet practical preaching style that makes corporate worship a more passionate and inviting endeavor.

Given that many black churches are successfully engaging young people, it seems ironic that these same churches rarely use contemporary versions of the Bible. In fact, the majority of black pastors have kept one major link with tradition: the use of the *King James Version* of the Bible. Our research shows that 7 out of 10 pastors of African-American churches preach from the *King James Version*. No other version or translation is used by even 10 percent of black pastors. This enduring relationship with the *King James Version* is a reflection of the importance of tradition in the black church, the high proportion of Baptist churches in the African-American community and the acceptance of the *King James Version* among the black laity.[20]

A major challenge in American churches is getting congregational members to *prepare* for corporate worship. Indeed, fewer than half of all churchgoers make any effort to get themselves mentally or spiritually ready before a worship event. Millions of adults consider their *attendance* at the event to be ample proof of their commitment to worship. This lack of preparation puts pressure on frustrated worship leaders to use their limited time and energy to direct people's attention to God.[21] Precious time is often wasted in services because worship leaders must cajole or coerce people into an attitude of worship. Simple investments, such as a commitment to Bible reading, prayer and devotional time, can prepare people for the awe of worshiping our holy God.

Despite what may seem to be shallow, emotional services to some, high-impact black churches appear to be cultivating a hunger for more connection with God. Significantly higher numbers of black adults read from the Bible and pray to God during the week. The inspiration and motivation they receive from meeting the living God in worship are a major catalysts for this brand of authentic spiritual engagement.

SOME BASIC STEPS WITH SIGNIFICANT IMPACT

Our nation desperately needs to cultivate a church culture that encourages life-changing encounters with God. We believe that the success that black churches have experienced in worship is attributable to basic steps that any church can take to make a difference in its worship.

The music in the black church is planned and performed with unique intensity. Not only is a lot of time spent but also many people are involved in the development of music that is designed not to showcase talent or make people feel comfortable but to help them eliminate all mental and emotional distractions so that they can connect with God. The preservice planning, prayer and coordination of multiple choirs, musicians and special program leaders require a clear focus and theme for each service. The result of focus, involvement and prayer is often a powerful encounter with God.

African-American preaching creates an atmosphere of

excitement and a hunger for listeners to seek encounters with God. Most Protestant churches have gifted communicators who know God's Word and do their homework in preparing theologically correct messages. Perhaps the major difference between the typical Protestant sermon and those delivered by high-impact black pastors is the combined sense of significance that black preachers assign to their sermons along with the practical, prophetic preaching style that answers meaningful questions in clear terms. In fact, one of the most eye-opening differences between white and black Christians is that the latter are much more comfortable diving into God's Word for wisdom, confident in their ability to study the Word. That self-confidence can be traced to the fact that so many of the high-impact preachers go to great pains to show their people how to rightly divide the Word.

Black churches work hard to remain contemporary and culturally relevant. Musical diversity and multigenerational leadership in the music department yield great dividends. It takes a lot of time and energy to mobilize these multifaceted music departments. Unlike many churches in our culture, the black church is still attracting youth and young adults without creating entirely new churches aimed specifically at that segment.

CHAPTER 5

EVANGELISM: THE GREAT COMMISSION AS A WAY OF LIFE

The mark of a great church is not its seating capacity,
but its sending capacity.
—MIKE STACHURA

In an earlier chapter, we noted that research consistently points out not only the similarities among Americans and how they live but also that blacks are more prone to seeing the world through the lens of biblical principles and Christian faith. One of the most vivid indicators of that perspective is the fact that at the beginning of 2004, a long-term pattern was still firmly in place: Blacks are far more likely to accept Jesus Christ as their Savior than are other Americans. Roughly half of the black population was born again (47 percent) compared with just 30 percent of all other citizens. That means black adults are 57 percent more likely to be disciples of Christ than are other Americans.[1]

Outcomes such as this do not happen by accident. And historical patterns such as this usually emerge from some type of cataclysmic event or enduring cultural distinctive. This is especially significant in the case of African-Americans and their faith. In order to understand high-impact black churches in twenty-first-century America, you have to grasp the history of blacks and how their faith has always been a central component of their world.

The faith of black Christians has been the source of many myths and controversies over the past two centuries. Some of the debate came to a head in the '60s and '70s, when militant blacks

Blacks are far more likely to accept Jesus Christ as their Savior than are other Americans.

began to attack Christianity as the white man's religion. They charged that American whites had stripped the slaves of everything, including their native religions, delivering a final, demoralizing blow to African pride by giving blacks a white god. The radicals even argued that Christianity had been used as an emotional pacifier by unjust masters who had selectively and hypocritically quoted the Bible, manipulating slaves through their faith in Christ.

Despite the popularity of the idea that whites seduced blacks into joining their religion, this view of history has little, if any, basis in fact. On the contrary, No Blacks Allowed signs seemed to swing over the entrances of churches for at least the first 120 years of the slaves' presence in America. Even though early colonial Christians rejected blacks, many African-Americans made the choice to follow Jesus wholeheartedly. Their zeal for God and their soul-winning efforts were so fruitful that some people believe whites must have brainwashed the early African-American elders. Black Christians of that era were not passive recipients of the Word. Indeed, a true depiction of the evangelization of African-Americans is a story of black heroism, tenacity and genuine faith.

FAITH JOURNEY

Muslims have been reported to be the early propagators of African slavery. Many slaves were taken to North Africa to serve as field hands, domestic workers and concubines. As European and western Christians got involved with the merchandizing of humanity, traders and owners rationalized the inhumane treatment of their slaves because they weren't Christians.

Upon the arrival of blacks in the colonies, some slaveholders began to evangelize their own slaves. As the small number of African converts grew, many Christians faced the challenge of how to relate to these new converts appropriately. Similar to the Early Church's question about receiving Gentile believers (see Acts), there was great contention as to whether Christian slaves should be accepted into full church fellowship.

When the Society for the Propagation of the Gospel (SPG) began to push for blacks to be accepted among American Christians, the move met strong opposition. The moral question of slavery would remain unanswered until the conclusion of the Civil War but during the early colonial period the rationalization for slavery changed from a religious argument to a race-based one. Blacks were simply declared to be inferior to whites. In fact, state governments passed laws guaranteeing that blacks would remain slaves despite their Christian baptism. Maryland pioneered such legislation in 1664, followed by Virginia in 1667.[2] Why should these state legislatures be so controlling and develop laws that seem so contradictory to the love, honor and freedom that the Scriptures describe? Similar to our nation today, such decisions were driven by the politics of influence and money. State governments wanted to protect their influential and wealthy citizens from losing the economic benefits of forced labor.

As early as 1715, a North Carolina law imposed a heavy fine on masters or owners of slaves who allowed their slaves to build on their lands "any house under pretense of meeting . . . upon account of worship."[3] In North Carolina, no slave or free black could preach or exhort from the Bible. More moderate states required whites to be present in black religious services.[4]

South Carolina was even more rigid than its northern neighbor—state law prohibited blacks from assembling for religious services *at all*. Slaveholders feared that if large numbers of blacks gathered without appropriate supervision, church meetings would become planning sessions for escape or revolt.

The black journey to faith was not an easy one but eventually religious restrictions began to ease. America's first Great Awakening (1740) was a turning point for the entire nation and it was during this period that the black masses were allowed to respond to outdoor revivals and camp meetings. As Americans of all races became born again, a desire to evangelize the slaves was one of the by-products of this movement. Many of the previous restrictions were lifted and blacks were eventually welcomed into the Christian fold.

In general, the temperament and the stiffness of "Northern Christianity" were not appealing to blacks. As a result, the conversion rate of northern blacks was comparatively low. All the major denominations in the Northern states were equally challenged. This is interesting in light of the fact that a hundred years later many abolitionists would come out of the North. Historians believe that the style of "Southern" preaching and worship services was more attractive to the slaves. Therefore, thousands of blacks living in the South responded enthusiastically to the person and claims of Jesus Christ.

As the zeal to evangelize every living creature grew stronger after the initial Great Awakening, church leaders experimented with many approaches to winning and discipling the black converts and the hearts of millions of white Christians softened toward their dark-skinned brothers and sisters in Christ. As early as 1743, the Methodists officially denounced slavery in their general conferences. As a result, large numbers of slaves were converted under the powerful ministry of John Wesley. His first two black converts were baptized on November 29, 1758. The first Methodist society did not begin until 1764, in Frederick County, Maryland, and African-Americans were recorded as being among their charter members. A woman named Aunt Annie, a slave of the Seitzer family, was a part of the first class.[5] Despite their conservative English backgrounds, the Methodists had a heartfelt, convicting style of ministry. The Methodists were not the only group evangelizing the blacks— Baptist groups had the greatest impact on the American slave community.

Early Black Churches

The first black church was founded in Silver Bluff, South Carolina. During the years 1773 to 1775, a white preacher we know only as Palmer began preaching to the slaves of George Galphin, a local slave owner. Several of the converted slaves who exhibited strong leadership gifts rose to prominence. George Liele and Andrew Bryan organized the first Negro Baptist Church in the American colonies.

After founding the church, Liele was sent to Jamaica. Like many converted slaves, Liele wanted to take the message of salvation to the entire world. These men often cited Psalm 68:31, *KJV*:

Ethiopia shall soon stretch out her hands unto God.

By 1793, this pioneer missionary had won 500 converts.[6] In Liele's absence, leadership duties at the South Carolina church fell on the shoulders of Andrew Bryan. From an academic point of view, he was an unlikely leader; he had to be assisted in reading by his brother Sampson.

To make matters even more daunting, South Carolina was not friendly territory for a black preacher. Andrew and Sampson Bryan were often harassed and persecuted for preaching the gospel. During one of their most harrowing encounters, both brothers were arrested and dragged before the magistrate. Andrew told his persecutors that he rejoiced not only to be whipped but would also freely suffer death for the cause of Jesus Christ. Andrew claimed to have been cut and bled profusely as they waited for the court's decision. They were mysteriously released from their nightmarish ordeal. Like the apostles of old, they continued to preach the gospel.[7]

By 1790, Bryan's church had 225 official members and another 350 converts who did not have permission from their owners to be baptized. By 1800, Bryan was able to worship without further persecution.

Meanwhile, the Methodist movement struggled to find the leadership needed to reach and disciple blacks on American soil. Francis Asbury, a British-born, white Methodist bishop who came to America in 1771, attempted to share leadership responsibilities with blacks. He was led by God to have as his traveling companion an illiterate black preacher named Harry Hosier. Hosier was marvelously used by God to lead many people to Christ.[8]

Unfortunately, these models of multiracial leadership usually did not work well. The baton for leadership would have to be passed to the black leaders themselves. Wise enough to recognize this reality, Bishop Asbury eventually helped to dedicate the building of Bethel Church in Philadelphia, which would become the mother church of a new denomination—the African Methodist Episcopal Church (AME).

Richard Allen, the church's founder, was a former slave who had been a faithful Methodist for more than seven years. He moved through the ranks to become a licensed exhorter in 1783. Three years later, Allen desired to start an all-black Methodist church but leaders were reluctant to approve a black to serve his own people. On the other hand, there was palpable tension whenever large numbers of blacks and whites worshiped together.

In 1787, Richard Allen, Absalom Jones and several others knelt to pray in a racially restricted area. As a result, angry white officials pulled them from their knees. In protest, the black worshipers decided to start their own churches. In 1794, Jones dedicated St. Thomas' African Episcopal Church and Allen dedicated Bethel Church later the same year. From the beginning, the AME Church was concerned with providing social service to people in need, developing an educated clergy that desired to instruct their people and reaching the world through missions.

Early black Christians were rejected by society, feared by some religious groups and often separated from natural family members because of the cruelty of slavery. It is not surprising that early black churches developed a strong internal sense of community. In fact, the motto of the black Christians could have been "United in Christ against the world." Perhaps adversity created a deeper faith in the lives of pre-Civil War black Christians: Jesus was their primary focus and advancing His kingdom became their primary task. Like the persecuted church of the book of Acts, they multiplied despite social pressure and endured the racial prejudice that accompanied their efforts to practice their faith freely.

How Blacks Introduce Christ to America

One of the more daunting challenges that most church leaders face is that of motivating believers to share their faith in Jesus with nonbelievers. This task is more readily accomplished among black people because they have a greater tendency to

Ideas without action are just dreams, and a culture is not saved through idle thought.

accept the role of evangelizer. Our 2004 tracking data shows that blacks are much more likely to assert strongly that they have a personal responsibility to spread the Word: Half of all black adults strongly confirmed that duty, compared to just one-third of all other adults. In fact, that ratio has remained constant for more than a decade.[9]

That determination to convey the saving grace of Christ is fueled by the reality that blacks feel regarding their own salvation. For instance, not only do more than 9 out of 10 black adults say their religious faith is important in their lives but 95 percent also claim that their faith helps them feel good about themselves and 9 out of 10 say their faith is a source of emotional strength.[10] Such a positive view of faith spurs many blacks to share their beliefs and experiences with people who are in a different place spiritually. In other words, many blacks are motivated to evangelize because they realize the magnitude of what Christ has done for them and how it has changed their lives by making the unbearable bearable and made the undesirable consequences of their own sin escapable through the salvation offered through Jesus Christ.

Ideas without action are just dreams, and a culture is not saved through idle thought. It is the determination of black people to translate their faith into action that has brought about the high proportion of African-Americans who are Christians, as well as the consistently high level of evangelistic activity evident within the black community. The 2004 study has revealed that nearly two-thirds of born-again black adults had shared their faith with a non-Christian in the past year, which was substantially higher (31 percent) than the slightly-less-than-half of non-black born-again adults who had shared their faith during the previous 12 months.[11]

The differences do not end there, however. The more positive efforts and outcomes are intimately related to different targets, tactics and messages in the process.

TARGET AUDIENCE

Blacks are a mission-minded people. However, their mission target is more narrowly defined than that of many whites. In America, blacks are intensely focused on reaching other blacks, whether in their homeland or in other nations of the world, whereas white churches in America seem to think of themselves as the center of the Christian world and thus possess a deep-seated sense of responsibility for reaching every people group on Earth. When black churches raise money for global missions, African nations are typically the recipients. When focusing on home missions, black churches usually give to urban ministries.

In like manner, when blacks think about sharing their faith, they are most comfortable and most likely to share with other blacks. The dominant emphasis is generally upon family members, including those outside the nuclear family. Because God's grace and acceptance are experienced as very real and unusual by blacks, there is often a greater sense of urgency about communicating the gospel to family members than is witnessed in other ethnic groups residing in the United States. Mothers emerge as the dominant evangelists in the black culture, constantly praying for and talking about the salvation of their kinfolk.

Outside of family members, blacks are most likely to assume an affinity for matters of faith with other blacks. It is almost as if African-Americans view Christianity as a faith experience that only they can truly comprehend because of what blacks have endured for so many years as a result of slavery, prejudice and economic disadvantage. There is much less concern about being deemed offensive for sharing faith principles or prayer with a fellow black than would be the case among whites or even Hispanics and Asians in this country. Because a sincere connection with God is still respected among blacks—even by many who do not have such a connection in their own lives—evangelistic efforts are responded to with greater appreciation and civility, even when the unsaved individual chooses to remain separated from Christ. The mere effort to bridge the spiritual chasm is still generally appreciated as a well-intentioned effort to enhance the nonbeliever's life.

Some Christians have observed this evangelistic segregation and noted that it seems inappropriate to be so color conscious about sharing the gospel. Our observation is that this is merely a practical reaction to the fact that blacks are nowadays accepted as sociopolitical equals by most whites and non-black ethnics but are not invited to challenge their existing beliefs, customs or values. It seems only reasonable, then, that blacks would go where they have the greatest chance of gaining a hearing for the gospel. This is perhaps a modern adaptation of Jesus' admonition to His disciples to remove the dust of a hard-hearted town from their feet (see Luke 10:8-12).

The Tactics for Outreach

Our research in 2004 has shown that blacks use a wide variety of approaches when they share the good news of Jesus Christ with others. The most common approaches used include praying for someone who needs encouragement or support; trying to live in such an overtly Christian manner that others are impressed and ask questions about the reason for that distinctive lifestyle; conversational or Socratic evangelism, in which one's conversation integrates questions about people's moral and spiritual choices in order to get them to think more carefully about their choices; bringing friends to church services or outreach events; and directly confronting someone who engages in an inappropriate behavior and explaining a biblical alternative to such behavior. Each of these methods has been used by at least 6 out of 10 born-again black adults in the past year in their efforts to bring the gospel to life for others.

Blacks differ from whites, Hispanics and Asians in their evangelistic practices in noticeable ways. For instance, blacks are much more likely to bring a friend to church with them (62 percent did so, compared to 47 percent of non-blacks). This reflects the trust and respect black people maintain for their church and its ministries. Members of high-impact black churches often bring friends to special events and services. Simply bringing a person to church can create an open door for sharing one's faith. Black exegetical preaching is often inspirational, encouraging and entertaining, a style that helps unchurched visitors see the value and relevance of church life. Further, the strategic use of altar calls seems almost universal in black churches. As friends and neighbors visit—often out of respect or courtesy to the member who invited and accompanied them—they may hear the claims of Christ presented in a new way or in a different context. Black churches tend to be less seeker sensitive than many white churches but the aggressive, in-your-face, roll-up-your-sleeves approach that black churches often take is likely to connect at a deeper level with African-Americans than would a prototypical high-energy, polished, polite seeker service.

Blacks are also more personally confrontational. A majority (60 percent) challenged the behavior of a friend or family member and followed up with biblical principles on how to behave in such a situation. (In contrast, less than half of all non-black born-again adults employed that method.) Black believers are also more likely than other Christians to engage in public witnessing.

Two-thirds of black adults indicated that they had engaged one or more acquaintances in a form of outreach that Barna first described nearly a decade ago as "Socratic evangelism."[12] In this process a Christian engages a nonbeliever in a straightforward, open conversation about a nonreligious issue that is important to the non-Christian. The Christian never implies that the nonbeliever is ignorant or uninformed. The believer attempts to avoid attacking the individual's views or conveying a holier-than-thou attitude, while patiently prodding the nonbeliever to clarify or explain why he or she believes what he or she claims to believe in reference to the issue under discussion. Such discussions invariably get down to a reflection on the source and content of moral and spiritual truth, which is exactly where an evangelizer hopes the conversation will lead. After several rounds of discussion, one of three outcomes typically occurs: The nonbeliever becomes frustrated with the process and disengages from further dialogue, the nonbeliever recognizes the futility of his or her position and changes or the nonbeliever gets frustrated enough to ask the believer to offer his or her opinion on the matter. The latter two outcomes are not only the most common but also the most productive. People converted in this way come to the conclusion that they need Christ—but the beauty of the process is that they see this as their own choice, not an alternative that was marketed to or forced upon them by a Christian. Previous studies have shown that these converts tend to be more zealous and committed to changing their lives because they were not manipulated into a particular view of the world.[13]

Black Christians often modify this method to stress their acceptance and affirmation of the person with whom they are dialoguing. This embracing and empowering approach to outreach is one of the best ways to reach young black adults.

A review of the variety of ways black believers share their faith demonstrates their relative lack of fear regarding the propagation of Christianity. They are not afraid to be personal, intimate, confrontational or bold, depending on the situation. While church events are part of the mix, blacks are less likely to rely on events as the means of introducing friends and family to Christ. More often than not, black adults are willing to roll up their sleeves and deal with the messiness of evangelism rather than simply usher their unsaved acquaintances into the presence of the religious professionals and hope things work out.

The Message Conveyed

The content of black evangelism is also a reflection of the uniqueness of the black experience. More than in other contexts, the message emphasizes hope. This reflects the great need in the lives of underprivileged, rejected and misunderstood people. Blacks have truly found a friend in Jesus, One who offers unconditional love and acceptance and these benefits have been the saving grace for millions of American blacks over the last two centuries. It is a message that minimizes the hardships of this life in favor of focusing on the glories to be realized in the next life, when we are reunited with the One who saved us. It is a message that the downtrodden find appealing, if it can be understood in its proper context.

Our observation is also that when blacks share the gospel, they do not get as hung up on theological nuances as do whites. They lead with their personal experience, which, in a postmodern culture that rejects absolutes but revels in individual stories, is a wise strategy. Like the blind man whom Jesus healed, many black believers cannot cite chapter and verse for their faith or persuasively argue from the Scriptures but they know what they have experienced and how freedom in Christ feels (see John 9:1-34). To their credit, they are too enthusiastic about their involvement with Jesus to keep the good news to themselves due to technicalities—they want others to have the same liberty and justice they have received.

EFFECTIVE EVANGELISM

Great evangelism does not just happen in our culture. Indeed, biblical evangelism is about as countercultural an experience as you will find. How, then, do blacks become equipped for effective evangelism?

The high-impact churches are tremendous examples of how effective evangelism works in a post-Christian society. Because three-quarters of all black adults contend that their church understands and addresses the most significant needs they deal with in their lives and two-thirds of black adults believe that pastors are the most important leaders in the African-American community and therefore give them the respect and trust necessary to accomplish meaningful outcomes, these are high-impact churches that have built upon the opportunity such perspectives provide. We found that there are five significant components related to how these churches facilitate effective evangelism.

1. Beginning with Leadership

As is true for so many things in ministry, impact requires focused leadership to guide people's efforts. That was certainly the case in the high-impact black churches and how they foster evangelism. With dozens of ministry activities vying for attention and resources, evangelism occurs only because the leadership of the church gives people the motivation and the means to establish gospel outreach as a top-priority agenda item.

Black pastors whose churches grow as a result of conversions facilitate such growth by making their self-imposed standard for success partially dependent on their church's evangelism quotient. This makes evangelism more than a program—it positions evangelism as one attribute of a healthy church that must be constantly assessed whenever the leader examines the vitality of the ministry. These are pastors who are not simply seeking people who applaud or are equipped to do evangelism but rather people who have incorporated the sharing of their faith with nonbelievers into the natural ebb and flow of their lives. Such a concept of outreach is one of the hot buttons of the highly effective pastors.

In fact, our research has shown that when black pastors, as a group, are asked to identify their top ministry priorities for the coming year, only two items were mentioned by at least half of these men and women: evangelism and helping people in crisis.

That forms an interesting combination because we also discovered that great black churches always join those two efforts together.[14]

In essence, the pastors of churches that revel in evangelistic growth have become champions of gospel outreach. They express that status through their preaching, the intentionality of their personal relationships with nonbelievers, their goals and evaluations and their pronouncements regarding the condition

> *People are not responsible for the salvation of others; it is the Holy Spirit who saves people and advances their growth in their relationship with Jesus.*

and future of the church. People take their cues from trusted and credible leaders. These pastors use their influence to communicate the centrality of evangelism.

What makes their efforts so intriguing is how they integrate evangelism into each of the roles they play within the world. These are pastors who wear multiple hats: civil rights advocate, community development leader, representative of the black community, religious spokesperson, spiritual model, organizational director, etc. Yet in each of these varied roles, these pastors find opportunities to bring their faith and salvation story into play. Perhaps this explains why black pastors fail to see any single emphasis as best describing their role. We discovered that about one-third of black pastors embraced each of several emphases as representing the heart of their ministry: connecting people to a bigger community of believers, inspiring them to accomplish great things for God, consistently growing in their faith and serving others who have discernible needs. Combining the multiple hats and the diverse emphases they pursue, it becomes easier to see how evangelism becomes a central focus.

It is the authenticity with which these pastors promote Christ that people find so appealing. Motivating congregants to be ambassadors for Christ in their families and in the marketplace is made easier by the seamless example pastors provide to the members of their flock.

2. Establishing Underlying Philosophies

The black church has developed a more refined ability to weave together disparate elements of the faith. While many churches operate in a compartmentalized, silo fashion, with programs taking on a life of their own and the ministry impact of any given effort isolated from the totality of the person's faith experience, high-impact black churches actively encourage their people to bring the various strands of ministry activity together for great cohesion and influence. The most striking aspect of this integration is the blending of evangelism, discipleship and service into a muscular brand of genuine transformation. Past studies regarding evangelism have led The Barna Group to note that "evangelism without tightly integrated discipleship is spiritual abuse." The study of black churches has revealed that they have brought this relationship between evangelism and discipleship to a deeper level by wrapping those endeavors around efforts to serve the most pressing personal needs of the individual.

The philosophy of these ministries includes the notion that people are not responsible for the salvation of others; it is the Holy Spirit who saves people and advances their growth in their relationship with Jesus. This is a very freeing notion—people are no longer burdened with responsibility but challenged with the privilege of leading people to the brink of eternity. This results in a churchwide perspective that churches do the best they can to plant seeds and it is up to the people to nurture them to the point at which the Holy Spirit can reap the harvest. Being part of such a team—self plus church plus Holy Spirit—relieves much of the self-doubt, fear and pressure that repel people from participating in evangelistic situations.

At the same time, high-impact churches achieve their impact not simply because the proverbial 20 percent is covering for the 80 percent in spreading the gospel. Great ministries are built on widespread involvement and high-impact black churches do what they can to foster in everyone's heart a sense of personal responsibility and privilege regarding ministry. The gateway to universal involvement is emphasizing that every adult has a duty to equip and nurture his or her household first and then to spread his or her resources outward.

3. Developing an Evangelistic Culture

Teaching and preaching about evangelism are not enough to get people involved in the process. We see that the great churches develop a culture that enables people to get it and give it. One central element is by recognizing that everyone has the duty to share God's love and that because it is the Holy Spirit who brings about the change in a person's life, no person is to be more highly regarded than anyone else for the number of success stories he or she claims. The true success, these environments proclaim, is simply the obedience to live like Christ and to share the good news when opportunities are provided. This type of culture highlights humility in obedience and service, making everyone comfortable that as long as they are doing what God has called them to do, they are a viable contributor to the Kingdom and its local expression.

Evangelistic impact is also realized by embedding outreach into every event and program the church offers. Although some people claim they get tired of hearing the offer to accept Christ as Savior, we found that black adults are less prone to such fatigue, perhaps because the offer is a personal reminder of the riches they have awaiting them in the next phase of life.

High-impact churches also reflect their evangelistic zeal through the types of staff they hire. In most cases, all members of the team, whether they are ordained ministry staff or uneducated support staff, have a passion for sharing their faith. This demeanor rubs off on the congregation and strikes visitors as special. It certainly gives birth to a ministry ambiance in which evangelism is as natural a behavior as taking an offering during a worship service.

4. Equipping the Saints for Multiplication

Like most Christian churches in our country, high-impact black churches offer a hodge-podge of evangelistic training programs and events throughout the year. The dominant philosophy of equipping seems to be "use whatever methods or strategies work and bring glory to God." There was little evidence of churches teaching people the one right way to share the gospel or criticizing unorthodox methods that have produced good fruit. Admittedly, even the most effective churches have to work hard to get their people to attend evangelism-training events. And while those offerings help many people to get their bearings, the two strategies that appear most worthwhile in enabling congregants to be effective evangelizers have to do with storytelling and prayer.

Blacks have a long history of oral tradition. Often kept from formal schooling, they learned to codify their experiences and pass them down through song and story. One of the natural offshoots of that history has been the ability of blacks to weave the story of Jesus, the rejected Savior, into their own tale of personal strife and redemption. High-impact churches encourage people to master their own story—and to be ready to share it with those who need to hear the encouragement that story represents.

Further, these are churches that believe in the power and the purpose of prayer. Having witnessed miraculous answers first-hand, many blacks have learned to lean on God during moments of trouble and to rely on Him for supernatural strength. That same reliance is evident in their fervent prayers for the salvation of individuals whom they know and whose souls they covet for the Kingdom. Consequently, you find evangelistic prayer in services, events and virtually every program—and even uttered between friends as they interact on the church grounds. Blacks are a praying people and they are quick to beseech God's help in reaching the unsaved with gospel. Prayer is a central element in the evangelism process of high-impact churches.

But there is also something to be said for the common focus these churches place on building a sense of community that provides the security to facilitate witnessing. The late black pastor Tom Skinner described the value of building up people's confidence and sense of solidarity in an evangelistic context:

> If we are going to evangelize our communities, we must develop those who are going to communicate the Good News. It doesn't make any difference whether you are going to evangelize in your profession, on street corners, in stadiums, or on radio and television. It doesn't make any difference whether you are going to do it through music, drama, or some other means that God gives you to convey it. What is important is that we develop a com-

radeship, a sense of family among the people who carry the responsibility of proclaiming Good News to our generation.[15]

5. Reinforcing People's Efforts

People pursue what they perceive to be valued. One way of determining value is to identify things that reap rewards. In effective churches, we found that evangelistic effort is rewarded. It has not even been the results of such efforts that have generated positive verbal reinforcement by leaders as much as people's courage to risk and their obedience to share their faith in any situation. The recognition given to those who make the effort comes in various ways: testimonials in worship services, affirming statements from the pulpit in reference to specific individuals or instances, formal recognition procedures, mention in church publications, etc.

As part of the motivational process, church leaders often recount dramatic conversions or growing numbers of baptized individuals as evidence of success. Those pronouncements invariably bring a wild shout of joy from congregants. It is that very celebrative ambiance that invites everyone to do his or her part in maintaining such an aura of effective and life-transforming outreach.

CHAPTER 6

CREATING GENERATIONAL BLESSINGS

The mind of Christ is to be learned in the family. Strength of character may be acquired at work, but beauty of character is learned at home. There the affections are trained.

—HENRY DRUMMOND

The current problems that face black families would have been unimaginable to the ancient tribal leaders of Africa. The idea that a black family would be unprotected on the shores of the North American continent violated every traditional value that those men lived by. How did the black family become one of the most publicly maligned institutions in America? It was not always this way but slavery had a destructive domino effect on the lives of everyone it touched.

The family was at the center of African life in the seventeenth century. Africans committed to more than lip service or verbal platitudes about their connection with kin. Their allegiance was to an extended family that went far beyond the nuclear family. Special honor was given to elders. Aunts and uncles were fiercely loyal to nieces and nephews. The tribe was a major source of identity. The roles of men, women and children were clearly defined. If tragedy hit an individual, there was an unbreakable lifeline that stretched from the individual to the family and the tribe. There was order and safety in the African concept of family.

These general statements would have been true in every nation of the sub-Saharan African continent in the 1800s. Although the specific customs would vary from Zimbabwe to the Ivory Coast, there was a universal value given to the family and its role in the world.

The best depiction of the deterioration of the black family was set forth in the Alex Haley's *Roots*. The best-selling book and blockbuster movie told the heart-rending story of an African slave named Kunta Kinte. One of the most powerful scenes of the movie showed a baby dedication ritual in which the young child was lifted high in the arms of his father and presented to the African gods. All the hopes and dreams for the family's future were wrapped up in this child. In this scene, Kunta Kinte was celebrated. The next segment of the movie described the elaborate training his tribe gave their male youth, which enabled them to enter into manhood and take their place in society. The rest of the movie showed the step-by-step journey of a free man into the inhumane world of slavery.

Roots told a story of paradise lost. The movie was critically acclaimed in its early days but its success left a bittersweet taste in the mouth of most black Americans. Black people yearned to know about their history and connection with Africa. For them, *Roots* was not just a history lesson. It emitted fact, fiction and emotion at the same time. For the first time, the corporate pain of blacks had a name and a face. Kunta symbolized the average black man's journey. Unfortunately, *Roots* had an incendiary impact on many people. Later, controversy surrounded the book's literary origins and some of its historic content. Despite all of this, for the most part, the book and movie accurately depicted the horrors of slavery. Slavery, as an institution, disconnected people from their tribes and traditions. As a result, their identities were lost. We are not simply referring to the loss of family names but also to the loss of connection with the internal family structures that assist every people group in achieving security and passing on their culture to the next generation.

This movie clearly depicted two major traumas of slavery that continue to affect black families today. The first trauma was that the spirit of the black male was broken. In his native setting, he lived as a dominant leader in a patriarchal world. By virtue of his maleness, he led and ruled his family with a benevolent hand of iron. His authority was often unassailable. The new world of America was the antithesis of the male slave's land of origin. Once in America the responsibilities of family direction, provision and protection were totally stripped from him. His status as head of the household was taken from him. A male slave had no authority over anyone, including himself. He had been reduced to a piece of "intelligent" breeding stock that could be used at the will of his owner. The other major trauma of slavery was that there was no protection for the children. Fatherless families under matriarchal leadership had no stability. The children were at risk both physically and emotionally. Black children had to grow up quickly and learn to fend for themselves in an abusive world.

THE CURRENT NATURE OF BLACK FAMILIES

The cumulative effect of the attack on the black family has taken a heavy toll from which it has never recovered. Let's consider the state of the black family today. Only 4 out of 10 black adults are married, yet two-thirds of all African-Americans are parents. Forty percent of black adults who have never been married have had children. Further, 9 out of every 10 divorced African-Americans have children.

The result of these marital breakdowns clearly affects the next generation. Only one-third of all black babies are born into a two-parent, married family. In other words, two out of every three newborn blacks enter the world with an unwed mother and no consistent father figure. The sad but undeniable truth is that most black children, whether they are born to an unmarried mother or are raised by a single mom after enduring the agony of parental conflict and divorce, are raised in less-than-ideal circumstances related to their moral, spiritual, social, emotional and financial environment.

The obvious question is, What triggers rampant illegitimacy in the black community? It appears that such parenting choices are a delayed reaction to the violent rearranging of families that occurred during and shortly after slavery. The reconceptualization of the family in African-American circles has been substantially affected by the American culture's recent moral drift. Years ago, blacks who married would usually stay together, even if their marriage was unsatisfying but things have changed. Among black Baby Busters (born 1965-1983), only 69 percent grew up with both of their natural parents compared with 80 percent of black Baby Boomers (born 1946-1964) and nearly 90 percent of those from the pre-Boomer generation.

These days, many black parents do not get married at all, preferring cohabitation, while a majority of those who do get married divorce before their offspring graduate from high school. The number of illegitimate births within the black community has always been staggering. Many currently married men in their 40s and 50s have had multiple babies out of wedlock. In an ethnic culture that has long accepted the fact that young children may be raised by their grandmother, uncles, aunts and other relatives, there seems to be widespread agreement that the nuclear family is no longer relevant.

The result of all these trends has been the disintegration of foundations that would otherwise facilitate family restoration. Consequently, less than half of blacks declare that their family is a safe place and three-quarters of the black families surveyed considered themselves to be financially disadvantaged compared to the mainstream community. Nine out of 10 blacks say that the black community would be better off if black men would take more responsibility in their families.[1] In fact, our studies suggest that 71 percent of black adults admit that the mother actually runs the typical black home.[2] The mother has the greatest influence on the dreams, priorities and goals of children—not by design, but by default. Until black men accept their rightful obligation to the families they create and willingly live within the framework of healthy relationship and authority roles ordained by God, the chances of seeing widespread positive change in black families is very limited.

The impact of dysfunctional families is most obvious in the lives of black children. Although 90 percent of young blacks say that one can count on God in case of crisis, one-third of black teenagers feel that life is not worth living; and black youths are more likely to report feeling stress, prejudice and a general sense of hopelessness about their lives. Our research suggests that while all teenagers struggle to adopt a realistic and appropriate self-view, that struggle is most intense among young blacks. Often, the developmental pressures with which they wrestle relate to the consistent absence of healthy role models within their household. Even as they strive to develop self-confidence and hope, their crushing environment leads to diminishing academic performance as well as an unfulfilling social life.

Without the strong and directive influence of a stable and committed family, the average black teen has too much free time, too little supervision and too many distractions. As a result, the family has not been able to hold the line on certain at-risk behaviors that threaten the lives and future of millions of black teens. By the time they graduate from high school, more than 7 out of 10 black teens will have engaged in sexual intercourse—a majority of them with multiple partners. Many will have experimented with drugs and alcohol, resulting in thousands of young lives twisted by abuse or addiction prior to graduation. One-quarter will have been arrested, thus starting their adult life with a criminal record. Such information underscores the dramatic erosion of the family within the black community.

THE CHALLENGING ROLE OF CHRISTIAN CHURCHES

In the face of such ravaging trends, Christian churches operate at a severe disadvantage. Given the history of the black family, it would not be far-fetched to note that it is miraculous that there are any intact, healthy families left! Indisputably, the depth and breadth of the challenges guarantee that matters will not be turned around within the span of a single generation. However, with the influence of healthy, forward-thinking black churches addressing these challenges, there is the potential to stop the erosion of black families and introduce viable principles and practices. We have learned that the leaders of the most effective black churches refuse to hide behind the veil of history; they exhibit their call to leadership by valiantly acknowledging and confronting these issues. Individuals must make new choices and churches must create new models that foster those choices.

Given recent social movements focused on abolishing the biblical foundations of marriage, the sanctity of human life and the distinctive roles and physical limitations of men and women, the Christian Church is perhaps the last ally on which the family can rely. Fortifying families is an uphill battle, even in areas where strong churches are present and active. It seems obvious that of all the dimensions of ministry and lifestyle we have studied, black churches are most significantly challenged when it comes to equipping families to be godly. Thankfully, there are more than a few congregations that have deeply committed themselves to this effort and are seeing tremendous results.

The most effective—though certainly not the quickest way—to transform families is to minister to one household at a time. Effective black churches focus on discipling parents, teaching them about their roles and empowering them to make a difference with their children. These churches face three major challenges in ministering to their families:

1. Making sure that ministry begins early in a person's life
2. Equipping each family to minister to itself, rather than to be constantly taken care of by the church
3. Refusing to accept easy answers by emphasizing community-wide solutions rather than individual responsibility

Let's examine each of these challenges.

1. Commencing Serious Ministry at an Early Age

Unfortunately, most black churches follow the typical ministry pattern in this country, which is to have what amounts to caretaker programs for children while the "real" ministry takes place with parents and other adults. The unstated philosophy is that adults can handle real content, whereas children need to be pacified until they are old enough to think and reason at a more advanced level. Adults attempt to use their gifts and abilities in ways that maximize their spiritual influence—and few adults perceive ministering to children as nearly as important as reaching out to their peers. This, of course, reflects what churches value: the presence and financial support of adults. Merely having a full slate of activities for children is deemed good enough.

Consequently, the unstated objective of ministry to children is to give them experiences that make them happy enough to want to return to church (and, of course, bring their parents), learn some simple spiritual information, make some friends and feel committed to the Christian faith. It is assumed that we need to prepare children for meaningful involvement in spiritual development rather than engage in such long-term development. Few parents understand the significance of the early years in a child's spiritual formation and few churches hold parents accountable for the spiritual shaping that occurs within the home the other six days of the week.

When parents and churches play this waiting game with children—that is, waiting until they are older, waiting until they can think more deeply, waiting until their behavior suggests they need a more sophisticated ministry—they forfeit the window of greatest opportunity for fostering spiritual growth. Young people do not need a holding period before the church exposes them to the real substance of the Christian faith. After all, the world does not regard age as a reason to hold back from reaching out to the minds and hearts of children. Ask any television network, marketing company or advertising agency if its strategy is to avoid children until they become adults or if they treat them as a viable market segment to be won over. They will lecture you on the naiveté of underestimating the decision-making ability and influence of youngsters.

Our research confirms the wisdom of investing respect and effort in ministering with vigor to children. For instance, we have learned that the moral development of children is largely complete by age 9. The vast majority of people who choose to follow Christ as their Savior make that determination by age 12. In fact, the probability of someone's embracing Christ as his or

The vast majority of people who choose to follow Christ as their Savior make that determination by age 12.

her Savior drops from 32 percent through age 12 down to 4 percent during the teen years and remains at just 6 percent throughout the adult years. Most people believe they know every major character, story and principle taught in the Bible by the time they reach the teen years. And we even discovered that whatever theological insights a person possesses are generally in place by age 13—and are not likely to change much, if at all, throughout his or her adult life. Even a person's impressions of church and decisions related to church attendance and involvement are largely (and sometimes irrevocably) formed prior to the age of 13.

It is for these reasons that it is imperative that churches begin to treat children as viable spiritual beings as early as possible. Even though most parents consent to the spiritual babysitting that occurs in many churches, it is necessary for the church to inform parents of the damage such a mentality creates and to prepare parents to work with the church in shaping the hearts, minds and souls of young children. When leaders, teachers and parents exhibit an attitude of complacency toward the spiritual development of children, they set everyone up for defeat.

For a church to be effective in ministering to the family, it must prioritize children and, in so doing, enlist the parents in a continual partnership. Even more than money, churches must devote focus and time to the spiritual advancement of their young people. Pursuing a well-conceived plan for what they want to nurture in each child's life is a critical undertaking—simply getting kids to return to church on a regular basis, telling them the same Bible stories over and over and enabling them to do fun games and craft projects have been proven to fail. What we build into the hearts and spirits of children when they are young is, in the long run, demonstrably more important than all the preaching, serving and relating that we facilitate among adults. Their spiritual foundation is shaped during their early years; we build upon that foundation, whether it is firm or feeble, when they are older.

2. Equipping Families to Minister to Themselves

Consider this reality: A church, on average, gets the presence and attention of a participating family for fewer than two hours each week. (We won't even discuss the fact that increasingly the typical churchgoing family attends just two weeks per month.) Is it reasonable to believe that during those two hours—a precious portion of which is consumed by administrative detail, religious ceremony and relational activity—parents and children will receive all the spiritual direction, affirmation and substance they need to grow and to represent Christ in our culture during the other 166 hours of the week? Of course not.

Unfortunately, most churches operate as if those two hours are enough to provide all of the spiritual nourishment and motivation that each person will need for the week. Families are seduced into believing that their church is doing everything that needs to be done in order for complete and comprehensive spiritual growth to occur, thereby releasing them from any spiritual obligation beyond showing up again at the next duly appointed meeting time.

The efforts of effective churches have demonstrated the folly of such thinking and have introduced means of equipping the family to minister to itself. It is not a church's responsibility to meet all of the spiritual needs of the family and those of its individual family members—that is primarily the duty of the parents, with the church lending support and assistance as necessary. Everyone within a family ought to be able to get spiritual nourishment as well as direction and skills for further faith development from the church but it is the family that will be held accountable for the progress each person in the family makes.

In the black context this often means that a reorientation of thinking and priorities needs to take place. For instance, recognizing that the vast majority of church-involved families are headed by a single mother, the church must assist her in becoming a spiritual leader and a champion rather than accepting her fate as a victim of circumstances. It means challenging the small percentage of black family men to support multiple families through mentoring programs without unrealistically burdening them with staggering levels of additional responsibility. And it demands that every person in the family understand the supremacy of the family as a place of spiritual development and encouragement, along with the responsibilities that are associated with that role. The African-American context requires some flexibility, since extended family members play such a prominent role in the upbringing of black children.

3. Emphasizing Individual Responsibility Rather Than Community-Wide Solutions

The black church as a whole is more often focused on bringing corporate answers to the problems of their community than on placing responsibility for growth where it belongs—on the shoulders of individuals and their families. Community-wide strategies designed by churches to impact family life through

You change the world one life at a time.

citywide or even regional activities are conceptually and logistically impressive but the jury is still out concerning the real effect of those efforts.

Community-wide strategies are typically long-term in their approach and incorporate various economic and educational thrusts toward revitalizing neighborhoods. Even though such strategies may be more attractive to funding agencies or individuals and are more likely to generate media coverage, the amount of resources needed to make a community-wide impact can be staggering. At some level, it may well require churches to band together to address bigger challenges related to social injustice and poverty. Such efforts are valuable and laudable but equal intensity must be directed toward strategies that focus on the families involved in the local church.

Indeed, the environment in which people, especially children, live and grow affects their capacity to develop. But we have learned that the most effective black churches realize a simple principle: You change the world one life at a time. You do not change the world by realigning communities at the macrolevel; you change communities by realigning the minds and hearts of the individuals who compose the community. Effective churches are active in citywide and even regional campaigns to create an environment that fosters individual maturity but their primary emphasis is on the individual and his or her family unit. If you cannot help an individual experience transformation, then you will not successfully alter the population at-large.

A Healthy Dose of Strategic Thinking

The state of the black family, as described earlier, can be disheartening unless it is put in perspective. If the goal of the local church is to meaningfully impact as many people as possible, then a healthy dose of strategic thinking is required. Our examination of black churches has revealed many examples of churches that have bucked the national trends in order to produce spiritually healthy families. Those efforts reflect the diverse, creative and adaptive nature of black churches.

Research has shown that the positive impact black churches have on families is related to the following six efforts.

1. Intentional Strategy
There is an intentional strategy with clear and measurable outcomes. Not content simply to pay the bills and keep people happy, these are churches that identify goals, create plans around the goals, hold people accountable for the execution of

the plans and regularly revisit the progress made in order to fine-tune miscalculations or unforeseen results.

2. Attitude Adjustment

These ministries realize that they must lovingly adjust the thinking of the people they serve. The idea of facilitating an attitude adjustment is a powerful tool among a people who are used to thinking that they begin every day at a disadvantage or whose resources are so minimal as to limit their dreams and expectations. Building on the biblical principle that "you do not have because you do not ask" (see James 4:2), effective churches recognize that progress demands intentional effort, and such effort is not poured into that which is considered unattainable. Even when the outcomes are biblical imperatives such as serving your neighbor (see Luke 10:27) or loving those who oppose you (see Rom. 12:14), a reengineering of the people's natural predispositions is critical.

3. Life Transformation

The most impacting ministries take a cradle-to-the-grave approach. The objective of these churches is complete life transformation, which demands an early start and a long-term commitment to each individual. The value of this multiyear perspective is that it facilitates an integrated approach to ministry development. Every ministry is related to every other one, across age groups and life dimensions, because each individual's spiritual perspective permeates every element of his or her life.

4. Family Ministry

Effective black churches understand the difference between equipping the family to minister to itself and substituting the church in place of the parents. A church can never succeed as a parental surrogate; it can only succeed when it strives to enhance the performance of the individuals whom God chose as the parents.

5. Motivation of the Congregation

The great churches offer moral support and encouragement in the face of long-term problems and overwhelming odds. Being black in America is not easy. Although conditions are far superior today compared with what blacks experienced 200 years ago, it is still difficult to break through and achieve a life of holiness and balance. Our culture has been aptly described as one of criticism in which our high expectations and competitiveness cause us to see the worst in others rather than the best. Effective black churches have embraced the role of motivating people to rise above their hardships and obstacles to accomplish great things through God's enablement. These churches help people to have the eyes to see the miracles that God performs in our lives on a regular basis. Providing a place of realistic optimism, hope and excitement in a world of despair, doubt and routine goes a long way toward enlisting commitment and earnest effort.

6. Identity and Unity

The most effective black family ministries work hard at maintaining a sense of tribal identity and unity. For example, both New Birth Missionary Baptist Church in Atlanta, Georgia, and Bethel AME Church in Baltimore, Maryland, see themselves as "a nation." This perspective is propagated through their preaching, slogans and leadership training. Both churches define themselves as a group of families and affinity groups (subtribes) that have become a miniature "nation" before God. In this context, a church is responsible to raise up leaders who embrace the membership in these huge churches as extended family members. These churches, and others like them, have successfully fostered a sense of belonging, identity and affirmation.

THE IMPORTANT PRIORITY OF YOUNG PEOPLE

Alert to the importance of relating to the minds and hearts of young people, many of the effective black churches have initiated ministry to black children and teens. Predominantly located in urban centers, these ministries have created new models for not only impacting individual lives but also seeing such transformation redefine entire geographic areas. In particular, we have identified five models that are adaptable to other communities, given the right leadership, commitment of resources and determination to persevere.

1. Community Outreach Model

In 1992, gunshots penetrated a crowd of mourners who were attending the funeral of a young gang member held at Boston's Morning Star Baptist Church. The crowd was stunned not only by the flying bullets but also by a horrifying stabbing of one of the mourners whose presence at the funeral was deemed a sign of disrespect by the attacking gang members. That incident, followed by several related homicides in the immediate area in the ensuing weeks, motivated a small group of local ministers to come together and commit to creatively and strategically reaching out to youth on the streets of their various communities in the Boston area. The plan they developed became known as the Ten-Point Coalition. The mission statement of the group:

> The National Ten-Point Leadership Foundation is a non-profit organization whose primary mission is to help provide African-American Christian churches with

the strategic vision, programmatic structure, and financial resources necessary to saving at-risk inner-city youth from child abuse and neglect, street violence, drug abuse, school failure, teen-age pregnancy, incarceration, chronic joblessness, spiritual depravity, and hopelessness about the future.[3]

Under the leadership of Rev. Eugene F. Rivers III, the leader of Azusa Christian Community, these courageous ministers committed to building relationships with gangs and drug dealers and developing relevant programs to redirect street-oriented youth. The resulting slate of activities included court advocacy programs, health center partnerships, neighborhood crimewatch support, gang-intervention programs, tutoring and educational offerings, evangelistic outreach events and a host of other initiatives. Working in partnership with law-enforcement officials, these churches were given a chance to confront troubled youths with a different alternative. Their goal was both to rebuild the lives of at-risk kids and to restore a sense of stability and community within the embattled areas of the city by engaging prevention rather than reaction.

Specifically, the Ten Points of the coalition are as follows:

1. Adopting youth gangs.
2. Sending mediators and mentors for black and Latino juveniles into the local courts, schools, juvenile detention facilities and the streets.
3. Commissioning youth workers to do street level work with drug dealers and gang leaders.
4. Developing concrete and specific economic alternatives to the drug economy.
5. Building linkages between downtown and suburban

churches and inner-city churches and ministries.

6. Initiating and supporting neighborhood crime watches.

7. Developing partnerships between churches and community health centers that would, for example, facilitate counseling for families and individuals under stress, offer abstinence-oriented prevention programs for sexually transmitted diseases or provide substance abuse prevention and recovery programs.

8. Establishing brotherhoods and sisterhoods as a rational alternative to violent gang life.

9. Establishing rape crisis drop-in centers, services for battered women and counseling for abusive men.

10. Developing a Black and Latino curriculum, with an additional focus on the struggles of women and poor people as a means of increasing literacy and enhancing self-esteem in young people.[4]

The process has worked well. The city's homicide rate—one of the most carefully watched statistics—dropped by 80 percent from 1990 to 1999, making Boston one of only two large cities that experienced a double-digit decline. Various cities across the nation have since introduced their own versions of this approach.

2. Family Life Center Model

Many black churches have created comprehensive programs that combine the use of extensive facilities with broad-based activities to support families from various angles.[5] Like the YMCAs of the nineteenth century, these centers offer activities, training and an extended-family environment for urban youth. Typically operated by one congregation, they allow young people from the broader community to interact in a fun and safe environment under the supervision of a leadership team from the church.

This subtle form of family and youth socialization was first pioneered by the Shiloh Baptist Church of Washington, D.C., under the direction of Rev. Henry C. Gregory III.[6] The idea was that the whole family would come to church directly after work or school. They would eat together with other families. Busy moms would not have to prepare meals every evening. Tired parents could actually connect with their own kids instead of expending all their energy on maintaining the functions of the home. A wide variety of experiences, ranging from recreational adventures to study halls and mentoring to more professional social services, were provided at the center. Studies of such Family Life Centers have shown their ability to reinforce positive family values in an environment of cleanliness, safety and excellence.

In some cases the level of investment required to maintain a successful Family Life Center has led a group of churches to band together to provide a cooperative center. Although the multiorganizational coordination effort can be somewhat draining, the benefits of such a joint effort have often outweighed the challenges. The Fayetteville Family Life Center in Fayetteville, North Carolina, is one example of such a collaborative ministry. Working with nonprofit service agencies and government departments, this center has fashioned a diverse menu of offerings that includes counseling and parent-education classes in conjunction with public schools, the county courts, day-care facilities and preschool centers as well as churches. The Fayetteville Family Life Center is credited with preventing child abuse and helping to strengthen families in the area.

3. Rite-of-Passage Program Model

The Jewish family traditions outlined in the Bible place great emphasis on ceremony and ritual. This is consistent with traditional African rites of passage to denote entrance into manhood or mature femininity. For example, in the Kenyan tradition a young Massai boy can only move into the ranks of adulthood after he has killed his first lion.

There are both biblical and cultural precedents for developing rite-of-passage programs in churches. Effective black churches understand that these programs are only as strong as the childhood foundation on which they are built. In other words, needy children who have not been adequately discipled prior to participation in these programs will continue to experience problems; these programs are not a panacea capable of negating the effects of traumatic childhood experiences or long-term spiritual neglect. However, effective churches use these rituals to help young people achieve an awareness of the opportunities and responsibilities related to moving into adulthood.

Upon graduation from a rite-of-passage program, participants receive covenant rings or other symbols from the church to remind them of their commitment to walk with Christ into this new season of their lives. Dr. Richard Durfield, Dean of Urban Ministries at Azusa Pacific University, pioneered the concept of giving covenant rings to his children as a way of encouraging chastity and faith in God's plan for their lives. What began as a unique strategy employed by an African-American pastor to nurture his own family has now become a model used all over the world.

A number of African-American churches use covenant rings in conjunction with the broader rite-of-passage training to nurture young people's commitment to spiritual maturity. The net result is that truths that young people should have been taught by their fathers are being instilled by the leaders of the church.[7] In addition, a passion for life-long learning and a determination to create their own spiritually healthy families are among the more common and gratifying results of these programs.

4. The Family Intervention Model

A different approach to building up black families through church-based ministry has been via the adaptation of intervention strategies. These efforts range from complex, foundation-supported child development programs to simple but sensible adopt-a-family projects.[8]

In response to the all-too-common anger of black youth, these programs create dialogue opportunities and one-on-one mentoring programs. The sponsoring churches realize that unless they intervene in the lives of the troubled children within their walls, these same children may become a menace to society because of the gaps of training and parenting in their background. Well-trained counselors working with parents and leaders approach these interventions as seriously as surgeons planning major heart procedures.

5. Church-Related School Model

While many churches in America have credibility when it comes to teaching about family matters, the black church in particular is viewed by its members as a desirable partner in training children, teens and family members. Because of the deficits related to family outlined earlier in this chapter, specialized training programs need to be developed to help make up for the vacuum in parenting and family training that exists within the walls of the nuclear family. One such strategy is to assist the family by providing Christ-centered elementary and secondary education.

Historically, black churches have not been as involved in

Christian schools as their white counterparts. This trend seems to be changing. We found that 7 percent of black churches now have an elementary or secondary school affiliated with their church.[9] While merely having a school available does not automatically solve family problems, a well-led school that requires continual parental involvement in children's education has been shown to produce astounding results.

THE CORE HOPE FOR THE BLACK FAMILY

Is there hope for the black family? Absolutely! At the core of that hope are strategically-minded black churches that marshal their resources to impact black children under 12 years of age. Just as the black church has always adapted itself to meet the unique needs of its people, the church must now continue to equip the fragmented black family to minister to itself. Many of the problems that confront black families today—illegitimate births, cohabitation, divorce, child neglect and abuse, the absence of role models—can be overcome by ministry efforts that target the youngest of children with the strongest of medicines: carefully planned, well-conceived, consistently executed and continually monitored spiritual development provided by parents in partnership with their church.

In addition to this strategic realignment of church resources, black leaders must be vigilant to protect their families from undue influence by the popular culture. Twenty-first-century pulpits must prioritize the value of family, fidelity and a clear Christian worldview. Because children, teenagers and young adults are targeted by marketers and non-Christian social activists, an entire generation of young people is vulnerable to seductive, unbiblical views on sexuality, marriage, relationships, family and basic morality. Today's black community as a whole seems to be unusually susceptible to the influence of well-marketed individuals emerging from the entertainment, fashion and sports industries. Black entertainers (particularly in the rap niche) and professional athletes vehemently object to being viewed as role models; some have made it a point to establish

> *It is God who established the family as His ideal means for nurturing, socializing, protecting and celebrating our progeny.*

themselves as antimodels. Their goal seems to be to get as rich as possible, while claiming no moral responsibility to their fans. Thug life, illicit sex and violence have become commercially profitable for black youth and young adults. In all of this, the worst aspects of black culture are typically the most celebrated.

It is God who established the family as His ideal means for nurturing, socializing, protecting and celebrating our progeny. And it is God who established the Church—the Body of believers working together to honor God in all aspects of life—to advance His kingdom purposes. The example of the black churches that have married these two hallowed institutions of church and family to create a powerful ministry force is a blessing to behold.

CHAPTER 7

HOLISTIC STEWARDSHIP

*We deem it a sacred responsibility and genuine opportunity to
be faithful stewards of all God has entrusted to us: our time,
our talents, and our financial resources. We view all of life
as a sacred trust to be used wisely.*

—MORAVIAN COVENANT FOR CHRISTIAN LIVING

Bible scholars trace the idea of stewardship back to the Old
Testament role of a manager who is responsible for taking care
of all aspects of a house (see Gen. 43:19, 44:4; Isa. 22:15). In the
New Testament, two different Greek words are translated as
"steward." The first word, *epitropos,* speaks of a custodian or a
guardian (see Matt. 20:8; Gal. 4:2). This word reminds believers
that we have been given many resources to watch over. Due to a
lack of perspective, many of us mistake the source or underesti-
mate the value of the gifts—spiritual, functional or material—
that the Lord has given us.

The other Greek word, *oikonomos,* deals with the management
of a house (see Luke 16:2-3; 1 Cor. 4:1-2; Titus 1:7; 1 Pet. 4:10).

When you merge these Old Testament and New Testament word pictures it seems evident that biblical stewardship is about the way we take care of the things we hold dear. As Christians, we prove how much we treasure the resources that God has given to us by guarding and governing those elements on His behalf. We are, in modern parlance, the estate managers of His kingdom.

The Bible also teaches that stewardship is a much more robust concept than we in the American Church have made it to be. True stewardship encompasses the supervision of every resource God gives us for Kingdom purposes: money, material goods, buildings, relationships, time, information, spiritual gifts and abilities, ideas and truth. So much emphasis is placed on raising and allocating money that we often overlook the fact that the most important resources are not financial—and that God will hold us accountable for the management of more than just our church and family checkbooks. In other words, most believers and churches focus on financial stewardship. Scripture exhorts us to practice holistic stewardship.

This matter in not insignificant—our choices always have consequences and God has alerted us to the nature of stewardship-related consequences. Jesus explained that if we aren't good stewards of our *earthly* riches, we will not be entrusted with the *true* riches and that those who prove themselves with limited resources will be given opportunities to utilize greater resources (see Matt. 6:19-21; 19:16-23; 25:14-30; Luke 12:13-21). The Lord's exhortations move us beyond worrying only about financial efficiencies to considering how well we invest *all* of the resources placed in our care.

STEWARDSHIP AMONG BLACKS

Focusing on the financial component of stewardship, the statistics paint a comparatively flattering picture of the monetary generosity of blacks toward their churches. For instance, consider the fact that in 2003 the average black church had a mean budget that was 36 percent higher than that of the average white congregation—in spite of the fact that the average household income of whites was 43 percent higher![1]

If we focus on a different aspect of stewardship—for instance, the time allocated to church-based ministry—we find that blacks are again more likely to devote time to church activities and service. When you combine the amount of time spent attending services, attending classes, participating in small-group sessions, being in church-related meetings and volunteering, blacks devote roughly 32 percent more time per week to church-based endeavors than do whites.

Even the time and energy devoted to discussions with friends and family reflect the heightened desire of blacks to do what is right before God. Compared with whites, Hispanics and Asians, blacks emerged as the ethnic group most likely to interact with others in relation to spiritual matters, moral decisions, financial choices and parenting challenges.

This apparent commitment of black people to using their accessible resources for religious purposes is not coincidental. Developing their stewardship abilities has always been a matter of survival for black churches and their people. Black churches during the early colonial days were poorer than even the most deprived mission field of our generation. The members of these churches had almost nothing to give. Can you imagine a slave's discretionary income? The income of blacks during the Reconstruction era was better but still meager. Despite their economic deprivation, blacks developed a culture in which caring for the needs of others and giving what little they had as generously as possible made a dramatic difference in their lives as well as in the lives of others. This ragamuffin mass of laborers, changed by the acceptance of the gospel and the strength and compassion that it instilled deep within them, quietly closed a seemingly insurmountable economic gap between themselves and other free men. It was such faithful and selfless sharing of God's resources that allowed the black community to establish an alternative economic system that incorporated savings and loans, banks and insurance companies. Their success was nurtured by the support of the black church.

We forget that when you have little, you are less prone to become attached to what you possess.

These days it is our tendency to admire the sacrificial generosity of blacks two centuries ago. But we forget that when you have little, you are less prone to become attached to what you possess. Documents detailing the ministry and context of Colonial-era black churches suggest that slaves had the advantage of not being owned by their possessions. They felt fewer inhibitions about giving away what little they had to others who experienced similar levels of deprivation. To some extent, that same sense of communal sharing exists in the most effective black churches today.

The Foundational Philosophy of Holistic Stewardship
Black churches have traditionally understood that it is not possible to facilitate holistic stewardship until people accept some fundamental biblical ideas about life. Genuine stewardship, they

reason, is dependent on recognizing that being created by God makes us special; that He never abandons those whom He loves; that "success" in this life demands surrendering everything to God and focusing on eternal things; that God's love and protection do not exempt us from hard times on Earth; and that our faith in the Lord is demonstrated by our behavior as much as by our words.

With such foundation stones in place, effective black churches then develop the finer aspects of practical stewardship. One of the most common perspectives we noticed is the emphasis upon living beyond the moment. This is perhaps best exemplified by the idea of teaching members to fish rather than simply providing them a fish to satisfy their immediate need. This concept originated with economist E. F. Schumacher concerning the empowerment of the poor.

> Give a man a fish . . . and you are helping him a little bit for a short while; teach him the art of fishing and he can help himself all his life. On a higher level, supply him with fishing tackle; this will cost you a good deal of money, and the results remain doubtful; but even if fruitful, the man's continuing livelihood will still be dependent on you for replacements. But teach him how to make his own fishing tackle and you have helped him to become not only self-supporting but also self-reliant and independent.[2]

Schumacher has only been partially quoted by many people. His philosophy goes far beyond just teaching an impoverished person to fish. The concept of teaching the poor person to create his own fishing tackle is tantamount to making him an entrepreneur. As part of the process of developing economic survival skills, Schumacher advocated training that is aimed at self-sufficiency. In order for people born into poverty to transcend their circumstances and limitations, there has to be a combination of information, hands-on training and the formation of new work habits.

In order to create "Christian" work habits, a person's character must be strategically developed. Such shaping involves changing the entire person, right down to how the person handles a checkbook. Churches that are committed to holistic faith—that is, the full integration of worship, stewardship, evangelism, discipleship and service into a full-fledged worldview and lifestyle that reflect one's faith—meet people where they really are, struggle with the most basic issues of attitude and lifestyle and get their hands dirty in the process. This is not a theoretical model; it is a pragmatic approach that reaps tangible outcomes visible in the spirit, character and business acumen of congregants.

This mentality helps to explain why there is a separate black business community addressing the unique needs of the black population. For more than two centuries, aggressive and foresighted black churches have been encouraging and fostering the entrepreneurial spirit of their people. Through the use of mentoring and apprenticeships, on-the-job training and investment in new works by the black community, progress has been made without the need to compete directly against better financed and highly credentialed mainstream businesses. The high-impact black churches around the country—such as West Angeles Church of God (in Los Angeles, California), Windsor Village United Methodist (in Houston, Texas) and Allen AME (in New York City)—have reframed the challenge such that they utilize the opportunities rather than becoming paralyzed by the imposing obstacles.

It Starts with Attitude

The ability of black people to remain generous as well as to skillfully manage a variety of Kingdom resources reflects an attitude of sensitivity to the Spirit. A number of Church analysts have concluded that black people, on average, devote more of their time, money and skill to advancing Christianity because of their knowledge of and commitment to the Scriptures, as well as their emphasis on the spiritual nature of life. Black adults are less likely to compartmentalize their faith than are other Americans, resulting in a richer faith experience and a very different expression of faith in their lives.

This tendency to view circumstances through a spiritual filter is not an attitude blacks have picked up from watching Fox prime-time programming or listening to James Brown records. It is a mentality that has been cultivated by the black church through conversations, sermons and ministry positioning that acknowledges the reality of the daily struggle without allowing hardships and barriers to define or limit people. The most influential black pastors encourage people to put their barriers in a larger, eternal perspective—neither minimizing the realness of existing challenges nor being hindered by the specter of difficulty, temporal failure or unmet expectations.

Stewardship Driven by Leadership

Holistic stewardship requires firm and focused leadership from a church. We learned that the high-impact churches have pastors and other leaders who encourage people to manage God's resources well because of the compelling vision of the future that they convey. While every church is called to pursue a unique vision from God, every church's vision is important in the development of God's kingdom. Each congregation plays a special role that results in transformed lives and that glorifies God.

One of the hallmarks of effective black leaders is that they do not focus on the wrongs of the past or the ills of the present but on the hope in a future in which Christ is exalted and His ways are preeminent. Our research suggests that while many people can give a stirring speech, the best black leaders are those who go beyond resounding words to deliver a viable notion of a future in which people can see their role and are willing to do their part. This requires a leader who is credible, competent, connected and courageous in pursuing change. We found that when such a leader invites people to join in a movement of faith, people are desirous of adding the value they bring to the process. More often than not, the leader guides people's ideas about how they can invest their resources in the movement.

Sermons and large meetings are the most widely recognized forums for casting such vision and motivation. However, we found that effective leadership requires a more hands-on approach to instigating great stewardship. Great pastors spend time interacting with people to determine how they can best use their resources toward seeing their shared dream become a pleasing reality.

In fact, we also found that high-impact pastors are well informed about the stewardship practices of their people. Surprisingly, most of the outstanding black pastors knew how much money each family was contributing to the church, which individuals were serving in some capacity, what special skills and experiences people possessed and they spoke very bluntly with people about the exercise of those resources. As one professor at a black seminary observed, "[Black pastors] call on church members to keep their covenant with God by supporting the church. . . . Unlike other churches, black pastors do know how much people are giving."[3]

Selling, Teaching and Modeling

To some degree, effective leaders are great salesmen: They sell the vision and the culture of the movement to their people. That is certainly true of influential pastors, regardless of their ethnicity. Getting people to abandon other worthy and appealing activities in favor of the church's ministry takes a good message that has been well communicated and backed up by accessible opportunities and constant reinforcement.

Stewardship is one of the areas that requires a strong pitchman and an equally strong plan of action for people to follow. The pastors of high-impact churches recognize that without resources, the vision they are promoting won't get far, so they seamlessly incorporate the notion of strategic and sacrificial investment in ministry as an alternative lifestyle.

Having evaluated thousands of churches over the years, it has become clear to us that stewardship can be developed on the basis of one of two things: projects or vision. Project-driven stewardship is useful but it is also short-lived. Once the project is complete—or, in some cases, no longer high profile—people's interest and their commitment deteriorate. Vision-driven stewardship, however, has longevity and intensity. Watch any great leader at work and you will most likely find that the bulk of his or her personal energy is devoted to getting people to own the vision and to prove that ownership is not by verbal assent but through the commitment of resources. Lasting, life-changing stewardship is best facilitated by vision-based calls to action and generosity. After all, people are more likely to retain their excitement about building hope than they are about retiring debt or constructing another building.

The most obvious way in which core stewardship principles and practices are fostered is through biblical teaching. Whether the lesson comes through a sermon, a Sunday School class, a small-group lesson or a letter to the congregation in the church's newsletter, the call to stewardship is a constant theme. Stewardship may be conveyed through very different theological frameworks. The churches may emphasize seed faith (see Matt. 17:20; Luke 17:6), sowing and reaping (see 2 Cor. 9:6) or personal consecration (see Josh. 3:5-13), yet there is a harmony of practical application. There are a few times throughout the year when these leaders will focus their entire message on overt stewardship (e.g., messages related to financial pledges, tithing, using one's spiritual gifts effectively) but more often the message is a subtle reminder that our responsibility as Christians is to bless others as we have been blessed. Such teaching provides two outcomes: instruction as to what a Christian ought to do in order to be a good steward and reinforcement of the commitment carried out by those who understand those responsibilities. One thing that black leaders intuitively understand is that a message people buy today must be reinforced tomorrow if it is to have any staying power. The marketplace is so highly competitive and people's focus is so diverted that any attempt at building momentum for a cause demands constant restatement and fortification.

Great church leaders take this a step further. We have recognized that the pastor and other key leaders often devote a lot of time to personal meetings with congregants. Often arranged around a breakfast or lunch, or sometimes a small gathering at a coffee shop, the leader convenes these private meetings to get face time with parishioners and ensure that everyone is on the same page and feels included in the push for progress. Although these meetings are time consuming, they pay enormous dividends. Laity feel emotionally and spiritually connected to their leader, their role within the ministry is clarified, their personal value is vindicated and their confidence in the leader typically rises. These leaders enter each conversation with a clear sense of the desired outcomes and use the time wisely to drive home the responsibilities and rewards emanating from each person's commitment to the cause.

Ultimately, the credibility and the influence of the leader are determined by overt evidence that the leader personally lives out what he or she is asking of the followers. All the face time and platform talk in the world won't sustain much energy unless people feel that their obedience and sacrifice is merely an imitation of the model demonstrated by their leader.

Interestingly, blacks are more lenient about pastoral modeling than are whites or Hispanics, largely because they realize that they must have a united front in order to make gains in the world, and that their pastor is the chosen leader who needs a show of unified support in order to have impact outside their church. Yet even in African-American churches we see that people's willingness to give sacrificially and to reorder their material priorities is at least partially dependent on the sense that their pastor is walking the talk with them.

When you observe the interaction between pastors and congregants in black churches, you will find that pastors regularly allude to their own acts of service and commitment. The late night or weekend meetings, participation in community groups and study commissions, efforts to develop good relations with lukewarm or hostile groups, leadership of community efforts to address poverty and injustice—all of these activities model stewardship as a means of cultural influence through faith expression. It is a more sophisticated way of envisioning and positioning stewardship. Merely raising money for ministry operations, as important as that may be, is not enough.

When it comes to raising money, we found that black pastors often orchestrate a knockout punch at the beginning of a fund-raising effort. Hoping to spur their people to confident and extravagant giving, the senior pastor will often majestically announce how much he and the other leaders of the church have committed to giving to the campaign. Such a show of devotion to the cause sends an unmistakable message to congregants: The leaders believe so deeply in the efforts being funded that they were anxious to be the first to give all that they can to see the plan through.

How do you motivate people to devote generous portions of limited resources, such as time, money and energy, toward spiritual outcomes?

As an aside, it is important to point out that when a church embarks on a fund-raising campaign—whether it be the annual stewardship drive or a special campaign for buildings, staffing, programs or missions—the senior pastor is generally not the one who spearheads that effort. In an attempt to steer clear of an image of "fund-raiser" or "money-hungry," great leaders leave the large-scale fund-raising to appointed lieutenants and simply give their blessing to the campaign. The senior pastor will meet with donors of large sums to stimulate such generosity or solidify such commitment.

Intentional Motivation

Many of the outstanding black leaders we studied are motivational masters. In American society we sometimes think negatively of professional motivators but a critical aspect of effective leadership is helping people to adopt and invest in a common vision for long-term transformation. Because the marketplace—even the church community—is filled with competing ideas and opportunities, and because most people are so stressed and fatigued due to all the choices they must make and all the responsibilities they must fulfill, motivation is not clever hucksterism but simply good leadership.

But how do you motivate people to devote generous portions of limited resources, such as time, money and energy, toward spiritual outcomes? Our research has shown that there are seven touch points that trigger people's investment. Effective leaders strive to satisfy as many of these as possible. Briefly, the following are the major touch points.

1. **Trustworthy.** Before people will part with their money, ideas, relationships or time, they must be convinced that the recipient of their resources has integrity. This is a fairly recent requirement, instituted in reaction to all the scandals occurring in ministry, business and government. In essence, people have laid down the challenge: If you want my goods, you must prove that your character and competence deserve my sacrifice.

2. **A shared cause.** The shared cause is the vision that drives the enterprise. People give away resources for all kinds of reasons—image, charisma, peer pressure, habit, tradition, selfishness—but the most robust and long-lived reason is a jointly held understanding of a preferable future that an individual's commitment can help to secure. Conveying that vision in ways that spark people's enthusiasm is critical to effective stewardship.

3. **Addressing urgent need.** People have been trained

to prioritize the urgent first and the constant second. When exhorting people to invest in the work of the church, help people to see the importance of achieving balanced giving—taking on the urgent needs immediately but leaving some resources in reserve for the ongoing needs that ultimately determine the success or failure of a movement of faith. Often it is the urgent that loosens people's reserve; it is the long-term benefits of pursuing the vision that fosters a lifestyle of stewardship.

4. **Intimacy with the ministry.** People hate to feel as if they are outsiders looking in. Ask any political candidate how he or she raises money for a run for office and you'll discover that it is by helping people feel as if they are on the inside of a revolution that is designed to change the world. Ministry is no different—people are sizing up the wisdom of allocating a significant portion of their limited resources to some parcel of actions designed to produce some type of outcome. The more that people can be made to feel that they are truly part of a single-minded, like-hearted community that is focused on a common ideal, the more they will believe that the entity is an extension of their life mission. Facilitating such intimacy entails facilitating and maintaining meaningful relationships within the church body, providing ample information about the direction and flow of activity in pursuit of the vision and having access to key individuals and resources related to the unfolding movement.

5. **Effectiveness.** Stewardship demands wise use of resources. One measure of the viability of a church is

the effectiveness of a ministry. People are loath to give their resources to something that has no impact. Black churches, in particular, seem riveted on the matter of making a discernible difference through the ministry: Simply *being present* pales in comparison to *bringing change*.

6. **Efficiency.** The other side of the effectiveness coin is efficiency—getting the job done well with the least expenditure of resources. Waste is the enemy of good stewardship. Great ministries help people to look for and recognize the intelligent and strategic use of resources as well as the minimal application of those resources to get the job done. Helping people to remain cognizant of these demands sensitizes them to the scope of the vision and to the need to conserve resources for maximum influence.

7. **Personal benefit.** This is not as self-serving as it may seem. People devote their resources to things that matter to them. In some cases, they invest in causes that advance personal as well as community interests: eliminating poverty, redressing injustice, expanding economic opportunities, etc. In other cases, they invest in outcomes that help people to whom they have a personal connection, such as relatives or friends. In either instance, their investment is a matter of pride because they are making a difference in people's lives in ways that are personally satisfying.

The more of these seven components a stewardship effort can satisfy, the more successful it will be at encompassing the time, talents and other treasures of the church's constituency.

Perks and Rewards

Many people feel that there is something wrong with rewarding people for what they are supposed to do. Over the years, we have encountered many churches that consciously, and sometimes vehemently, reject the idea of demonstrating appreciation for what people are scripturally called to do.

High-impact churches, however, make no bones about demonstrating gratitude to those who sacrificially pour themselves into ministry. There are all kinds of perquisites and rewards given to such people. In some cases the rewards are simple: words of thanks from the pastor, a letter of appreciation or commendation from the leadership or a plaque certifying the person's esteemed contributions. In other situations there may be a more public outpouring of gratitude: a word of thanks from the platform during weekend services, a flattering article in the church newsletter or an appreciation dinner in honor of the person. There are some instances, of course, in which the magnitude of an individual's investment justifies a more substantial and long-term remembrance, such as naming a building after a major donor or naming a library or classroom after an individual whose long-term commitment has made a massive difference.

There are more subtle perks, too. Giving people a title or position affirms their efforts. Providing them with access to classified information or to key leaders is another.

One of the most ethnically unique practices of black churches in this regard has to do with the recognition of reliable financial supporters. Some of these churches stage ceremonies in which tithers march down the center aisle of the church as they give their offerings during the worship service. Other churches create a Champions Roll, which is a public list of the people who faithfully give at least 10 percent of their income. Perhaps because blacks have rarely had much money, their churches seem less reluctant to talk about the generosity of members who devote a good portion of their earnings to ministry.

Regardless of the methods used, the underlying purpose is the same: to encourage everyone to see such stewardship as a praiseworthy duty of every responsible Christian. These rewards are a subtle form of accountability: The provision of such a reward reflects the faithfulness of the believer.

PHILOSOPHY ON FINANCES

Blacks churches have pulled off a virtual miracle by funding their ministries even more effectively than white churches. They have sustained people's giving despite having been the social outcast or underdog for so many years. Black leaders have certainly enlisted financial support and physical effort through consistent allusion to that status but the ability to sustain such stellar giving is what strikes us as so astounding.

How has this consistency been achieved? It has occurred because good stewardship habits have been formed in the lives of millions of black people. While this is not the norm in all black churches, the high-impact black churches have facilitated consistent and generous investment of time, money and abilities because they have created a culture that expects and rewards such sacrifice.

These are churches whose foundational philosophy of resource application has raised people's level of trust and confidence. We have seen that these churches foster good financial practices in people's lives and reinforce those practices through the ways in which the church ministers. Practically speaking, high-impact churches demonstrate excellent internal financial systems and cash-management procedures, good savings and investment habits and wise investing of funds in productive ministry due to sufficient preparation and evaluation of the ministry efforts supported. Churches train their people—through preaching, teaching, seminars and counseling—how to manage their personal resources. Then they reinforce those lessons by utilizing the very same principles and practices in the management of the church.

High-impact churches also develop systems that foster good stewardship. A classic example is the spread of investment clubs to teach church members how to save and manage their money. Many churches initiate these clubs at the middle or high school level and then offer them for all age groups, through advanced adulthood. Black churches use these clubs to help people capture the fundamental concepts of good stewardship in a free enterprise system. Building on the insight gleaned by wealthy whites (i.e., children take a greater interest in the stock market if they own stock), these church-based investment clubs are applying that core principle to help both young and older blacks become more financially savvy.

The financial philosophy of influential black churches also includes their operating practices. For instance, while many black families struggle with personal debt—black adults are more than twice as likely as white adults to describe themselves as struggling with serious debt—high-impact black churches stand out as having low debt ratios and a distaste for long-term, high-dollar financial obligations. Many of these churches take great pride in either raising all of the money for their building projects prior to the initiation of construction or getting minimal mortgages that can be paid off through accelerated payments, culminating in a mortgage-burning ceremony. Authors Eric Lincoln and Lawrence Maniya, in their classic book *The Black Church in the African American Experience*, observed that most black churches fully own their buildings and property, mortgage-free—a level of financial freedom that is rare among institutions in American society.[4]

Through their staffing practices, black churches further exemplify holistic stewardship. High-impact black churches have a tendency to grow more rapidly than the norm. However, numerical growth does not automatically result in building up personnel. The pattern seems to be that these churches strive to fill ministry positions with laypeople first, devoting resources to the training and equipping of those individuals for ministry success. At some stage, when full-time personnel are required, lay volunteers will be asked to become paid staff members—after they have clearly paid their dues and proven their merit. If any volunteer chooses not to join the staff or if a staff position cannot be filled through volunteer efforts, then the church expends its funds on a full-time ministry professional.

Further, we have learned that high-impact churches remain effective because their financial philosophy is realistic about what it takes to usher in transformation. Often ministry professionals think that ministry can be done "on the cheap"—expending few, if any, financial resources to get a quality job done. This philosophy may work for a while—but it may also backfire by burning out people, leaving them feeling exploited or by producing outcomes that are not of sufficiently high quality to make a difference. High-impact ministries "count the cost"— they know roughly what it will take to do the job right, and they plan accordingly.

It must also be noted that these churches are impressive in their balance of intuition and planning. Many of the great leaders we have studied are effective because they have a finely tuned instinct about what will work in a given situation. Rather than constantly shooting from the hip, they interact with their team of leaders and ministers to develop plans that build on those instincts and strategically incorporate people into the plan and resulting activity.

One of the most intriguing aspects of the stewardship endeavor of these churches is their commitment to transparency. Most American churches are very protective of their financial records, preventing congregants from examining the books at will. High-impact churches believe that accountability demands openness, so they allow active members of the church regular access to any financial documents related to the ministry.

Why do these churches go this far? Because they are modeling the essence of good stewardship: Never do things in secret, never hoard your resources, always be open to constructive criticism and be ready to give a defense for the choices you have made based on the principles that fostered those choices. Pastors can preach these principles forever but until people experience these ideals in practice they sound too theoretical. Opening the church file cabinets and checkbooks for member inspection sends an impressive and indelible message to congregants: Get your house in order and invest your God-given resources in a way that stands up to scrutiny and advances His purposes.

HEART OF BELIEVERS

The Christian community is divided on the issue of tithing. Some churches believe that it is a core biblical teaching; others contend that it is legalistic, a part of the Old Covenant that reflects the law more than the spirit of the law.

Regardless, the fact is that few American Christians donate at least 10 percent of their money—much less other resources—to ministry. Nationally, the 2003 data showed that just 3 percent of all adults and a mere 6 percent of born-again adults tithed.

The figures are not much more compelling regarding the black community. Overall, just 4 percent of blacks tithed—virtually all of these tithers were born-again blacks. However, among born-again African-Americans, only 8 percent gave 10 percent or more of their earnings to Christian endeavors.

Whether we focus on white, black, Hispanic, Asian, Native

Never do things in secret, never hoard your resources, always be open to constructive criticism and be ready to give a defense for the choices you have made.

American or other ethnic groups, tithing is not an accepted practice. (We do find, by the way, that more than three times as many churchgoers claim they tithe as actually do so. Whether this is because they misunderstand what tithing means [i.e., regular offerings], because they hope to portray themselves in a more favorable light or for some other reason, the bottom line is that the failure to give a rather minimal proportion of one's finances to God's work speaks to the true heart of most believers.)

When we consider the development of holistic, biblical stewardship practices in people's lives, the bottom line is not a percentage given as much as an attitude about and a commitment to our spiritual responsibilities. While high-impact churches fare slightly better in raising up tithers, the majority of churches in our country are still fighting against a heart that hoards God's riches for selfish purposes—no matter what skin color dominates the congregation.

CHAPTER 8

SERVING THE COMMUNITY

Preach the Gospel at all times; if necessary, use words.
—COMMONLY ATTRIBUTED TO SAINT FRANCIS OF ASSISI

A major Internet service provider posted an online survey that asked, Why haven't you pursued your dream career? Among the many response options was "not having enough money to get started." Over two-thirds of the respondents selected that option as their reason for not having sought to make their personal vision a reality.

The early African-American church could have stated that its lack of resources prevented it from being God's instrument of change for its members and society. Instead, the black church arrived at the same outlook that Thurgood Marshall, our nation's first black Supreme Court justice, adopted in reference to his groundbreaking achievements and unique vision when he humbly declared, "I did what I could with what I had," when a reporter asked him what he wanted to be known for.[1] Perhaps Marshall understated his brilliance but his unassuming response emphasized the essential role of perseverance. Through many years of diligence, the black church has developed an amazing ability to impact its environment and raise the quality of life of its members. By combining the individualistic boot-straps philosophy (you can do anything you put your mind and heart into) with a strong tribal philosophy (together we are stronger than when we try to do things in isolation), high-impact black churches have concocted a distinctive and impressive capacity for helping people get on their feet and focus on God's purposes for their lives.

A History of Helping

During slavery, Southern black churches had no resources or physical assets, yet somehow viable churches were founded and sustained. In the North, freedmen either established churches or mutual aid-benefit societies (which typically led to the formation of black churches). When slavery ended, many blacks actually settled near their former plantations. Churches and their pastors were usually at the very heart of these new communities. More often than not, the first buildings constructed by these new communities were church facilities. The impact of those churches upon society is usually overlooked. Black churches not only provided people with spiritual comfort and hope but they also established an economic support system that served as the precursor to government welfare agencies and nonprofit aid organizations.[2]

As theologian C. Eric Lincoln has pointed out, the black church played a catalytic role in the economic advancement of blacks. One strategic contribution was the church's involvement in creating the first major black financial institutions: banks and life insurance companies. In 1865, Congress chartered the

Freedman's Savings and Trust Company. Many believe that this bank held most of the savings of the newly freed African-Americans. Eventually the bank failed because of a combination of poor management and the national recession of 1873.

Most investors were devastated by the bank collapse. This event set black economic development back for many years. When the time was right to venture into the economic world again, church-related burial societies and fraternal orders became the springboard for the first black insurance agencies at the end of the nineteenth century and the early twentieth century. The church emerged as a credible bridge to future financial power for financially cautious former slaves and their descendants. One major company was the African-American Industrial Insurance Society of Jacksonville, Florida, which began in a black Baptist church in 1901. Soon thereafter the Penny Savers Bank was started in Birmingham, Alabama, by the pastor of another Baptist church. Foreseeing the need to protect black financial interests while positioning the church as a trustworthy and helpful institution, numerous African-American pastors followed suit, opening banks such as the True Reformer's Bank, the Galilean Fisherman's Bank and St. Luke's Bank.

There were myriad other institutions that faithfully helped African-Americans build lives of economic freedom, community by community. Unfortunately, the Great Depression wiped out many of them.

Overcoming the devastation of the Great Depression was no easy task. Thankfully, new heroes arose to meet the challenge in the 1930s. Some black churches held classes on the fundamentals of job seeking and household economics for people who had migrated from the South to the North. A great example of this was Dr. Robert Wesley Morgan, who worked in Poughkeepsie, New York. Dr. Morgan was a black dentist and an AME Zion layman. In 1936, he taught classes in both Catherine Street AME Zion Church and Ebenezer Baptist Church in his city. Behind the scenes, he and a coalition of pastors worked as a unified front to negotiate access for black people to jobs in hospitals, stores and even schools. These jobs had been closed to blacks prior to that time.

Authentic Christian ministry is never eliminated by money but is more often devastated by a lack of vision, courage and determination.

W. E. B. DuBois, widely acclaimed as a visionary for African-American unity and social empowerment, stated emphatically that any strategy to develop economic cooperation among blacks had to begin with the church.[3] The struggles and obstacles they overcame in the past have paved the way for the quality of life many African-Americans enjoy today.

THE PRIORITIES OF TODAY

The easiest excuse for avoiding confrontation with the Goliaths of poverty, crime, drug abuse and teen pregnancy that stalk urban America would be to complain about the absence of sufficient money. However, authentic Christian ministry is never eliminated by money but is more often devastated by a lack of vision, courage and determination. Today's churches certainly do not lack opportunities for ministry. In fact, America's need for the Church has never been greater. Sticking close to God's vision will help churches determine appropriate priorities and avoid the seductive mistake of trying to be all things to all people, becoming virtually useless to everyone because of being stretched too thin or straying too far from the heart of God's vision.

The black community contains a potpourri of socioeconomic realities. Black adults range from the very wealthy to the dirt poor—circumstances are improving for blacks but the balance still tips toward the less affluent end of the continuum. Consequently, black churches are recognized as places where the basic necessities of life—food, clothing, shelter and health care—are provided to those who are needy. Given their heritage as innovators and as suppliers of opportunities that address material needs, African-American pastors admittedly struggle with the desire to accomplish more than their resource base permits. But we also have discovered that unlike some churches, these congregations have less hesitation when it comes to working with government agencies and nonprofit organizations to produce positive results in people's lives. To them, arguments about separation of church and state or concerns regarding project leadership and structure pale in importance compared to helping people solve vexing life problems. Perhaps because the constituency with which they work is more desperate, these churches are willing to surrender some degree of control in order to alleviate people's suffering more quickly. Pride of ownership rarely compromises their determination to facilitate life transformation.

The Barna Group's study of African-Americans and their faith has revealed that there are a handful of priorities that represent the dominant social-welfare thrust of black churches. A church focus on economic development and related community welfare efforts is an unambiguous hallmark of high-impact churches. While a large share of the nation's white Protestant churches emphasize the importance of global missions as their primary form of other-centered outreach, effective black churches are more likely to stress the importance of impacting their own community.

It is important to note that these churches are major facilitators of the idea that we grow spiritually by getting our eyes off ourselves—what we need, what we want, what we're suffering through—and on to other people. The teaching in these churches reinforces the notion that Christians are servants, but that

> *We grow spiritually by getting our eyes off ourselves—what we need, what we want, what we're suffering through—and on to other people.*

such a notion is mere theory until we actually serve other people. It is not unusual to find very young children regularly participating in the church's service projects as part of their ministry training and lifestyle development.

A clear indicator of the importance of community service ministries is the unusually high percentage of black pastors who listed efforts such as helping people in crisis and community outreach as top ministry priorities. (More than two-thirds of all black pastors listed such concerns.) Other community-focused ministries that are widely prioritized include helping the elderly and reaching out to needy children and their families.

The research has also identified the most frequent ways in which black churches attempt to help people in crisis. The most common tactic is by providing food, a ministry in which more than one-quarter of all black churches engage. Other common, crisis-oriented services include ministering to prison inmates, supplying clothing to the poor, assisting people recovering from addictions and providing housing for the homeless. Not all community services focus on alleviating life crises. Most African-American churches recognize the importance of helping children and families remain safe and secure. Numerous family-oriented forms of assistance are offered, ranging from after-school tutoring, foster care or day care to skills training classes and counseling. One of the most difficult aspects of building and maintaining a strong community has been the intransigence of black men in accepting their appropriate family responsibilities. Just over one-third of black pastors (36 percent) believe that black men are carrying their fair share of family responsibilities. High-impact churches recognize the necessity of helping black men accept their role as the spiritual leader of their household, to address their obligations regarding their economic and political roles and to partner with their church in exerting positive influence upon society.

A more traditional form of family care includes the many activities related to elder care. Hospital and shut-in visitation, spiritual nurture provided in nursing homes and other types of encouragement and assistance provided to the elderly are quite common. This emphasis is a reflection of the respect given to older people; blacks have a deep respect for their aged parents, especially their mothers, and are somewhat more likely than people from other population groups to view this type of outreach as a mark of compassion.

The most prolific form of community service undertaken by black churches is facilitating racial reconciliation. Four out of 5 black churches (78 percent) are currently involved in special efforts to bring about understanding and harmony among the different racial and ethnic groups. This is one of the ways in which the black population sees churches playing a redemptive role in society while simultaneously easing the hardships associated with being a minority in America. Perhaps as a means of modeling the talk, as well as seeking ways to constructively and strategically enhance our culture, 6 out of 10 black churches (59 percent) are currently involved in a partnership or cooperative ministry effort with a predominantly white church or group of churches.

Given the history of blacks in America and the role the Church has played in their struggle to experience freedom and equality, it is not surprising to see just how significant community outreach is within the typical black church. Teaming outreach ministry with a heavy focus on evangelism often proves to be an effective one-two punch by developing relationships and credibility, strategically using resources and delivering tangible benefits to those in need.

THE ROLE OF PASTORS

Our research data indicate that most African-Americans—including those who are not presently involved in a church—view the black church as their representative in society. With that in mind, most black pastors have carefully considered the opportunities, the obstacles and the historical precedent related to the church's ministry and mission.

Most black pastors see their role and that of their church as a threefold challenge: providing the black community with a political voice and leadership, with social services and with spiritual leadership and services—in that order of importance. There is little wonder why so many community activists have emerged from the ranks of the black clergy. To black citizens, because justice and freedom are central biblical values, it is only natural to expect their religious leaders to work toward the achievement of those values in society. Consequently, relatively few black adults harbor significant concerns about the harmful mixture of religion and politics or the inappropriateness of having church leaders provide leadership in political arenas.

For their part, black pastors know they are relied on to be a black presence in the white-dominated world of policy making, legal matters and public discussion. They therefore see themselves as primary defenders of the rights of blacks and as social reformers. Racial reconciliation is just one issue they address but it is a key issue of their agenda. To be effective, these leaders realize they must have an overtly unified constituency or run the risk of not being taken seriously by society's power brokers. Therefore, the means to their end is to build community among blacks—a network of relationships that serves multiple purposes, one of which is to support the political maneuvering that accompanies social progress. Black pastors unashamedly portray themselves as political power brokers to be contended with and relatively few of their parishioners would criticize that emphasis.

Black pastors have a spiritual agenda, to be sure, but in most cases it is impossible to separate that agenda from the political and service responsibilities they embrace.

A CHANGE OF AGENDA

One of the interesting characteristics of high-impact churches is their ability to read the local culture and intuitively shift their ministry activity to address existing needs. This is readily evident in relation to the social and economic services provided through the church. As the black population has become better educated and more affluent, these churches have altered the menu of services they offer to reflect the changing needs of the community and the congregation. We have seen that the mentality is one of retooling the services offered rather than eliminating the funds and man hours allocated to community service; this type of outreach is such an ingrained part of the philosophy of ministry that the notion of transferring the same resources to ministry that is more inwardly focused does not seem to arise as a possibility.

These churches have also retained a healthy balance of resource provision and spiritual motivation. We have seen too many examples of churches that initially offer faith-based social services that eventually become more like religion-free government agencies in their processing of people and their needs. To their credit, the high-impact churches have such a strong spiritual anchoring that everything they do is overtly connected to their faith in Christ and their adherence to the Bible. When a person receives services from these churches, no matter what the benefit or value of the service, a faith component is inevitably associated with what they get.

These churches are so influential as sources of God's love, mercy, compassion and assistance because they never let the program become an end in itself. Their vision and their motivation for service remain pure and undefiled.

CHAPTER 9

RELATIONSHIPS THAT CHANGE LIVES

If you do not join in what the church is doing, you have no share in this Spirit. . . . For where the church is, there is the Spirit of God, and where the Spirit of God is, there is the church, and every kind of grace.

—IRANEUS

In the African-American community, entertainers, politicians, ministers and even sports figures have a very important function as role models and folk heroes. Positive role models have often been held up to contradict negative racial stereotypes concerning the aptitude, ability or character of black Americans. However, the prolific use of high-profile individuals as role models can cut both ways, as we have frequently witnessed in recent years.

Americans have become accustomed to hearing the disappointing news of the moral corruption or compromise of prominent spokespersons. In the past five years alone, we have endured a flood of allegations and courtroom antics regarding the alleged immoral or illegal behavior of corporate CEOs, clergy, teachers, professional athletes, entertainers and even a sitting United States president. Such scandals have become an expected part of public life in the twenty-first century.

The arrest of Washington, D.C.'s mayor Marion Barry in 1989 was just such an incident. A shrewd and powerful political official, Barry was videotaped using drugs with a former mistress. Although the mayor had often been accused of corruption, many months of investigations had yielded nothing that would stand up in a court of law. As a last resort, the authorities had arranged the illicit reunion between these two people in order to finally get something on the elusive Barry.

Charges that the sting had been racially motivated rang out across the nation. Some members of the press congratulated law-enforcement officials for their tenacious pursuit of a corrupt leader. After all, they pontificated, the man was caught on videotape, in the act of breaking both legal and moral law. In their view, the case was open and shut.

In contrast, black sympathies for Barry ran high because of his track record of community activism and concern for the little guy. The fear many citizens expressed was that there was a double standard for black politicians. Barry's white colleagues were probably guilty of equal or worse private indiscretions, the black public reasoned. The enormous expenditures used to entrap one man seemed to suggest that Barry's race had made him a target. His pursuers seemed like big game hunters who were eager to mount his political head as a trophy on their office wall, paving the way for future promotions and notoriety.

A casual observer would have assumed there was little hope for the mayor's political survival. Faced with felony charges and the prospect of a lengthy prison term, the mayor enlisted the aid of the district's most effective albeit flamboyant attorney, Kenneth Monday. In the months that followed, it seemed as if every legal trick in the book was being exhausted.

In the end, the unthinkable happened: Barry got off with just a misdemeanor charge. Most amazing was that Barry was reelected as mayor after having missed just one term in office.

How did this reversal occur? The answer is simple: through the unexpected influence of the black church.

> *The black church places an extraordinarily high value on giving even the worst sinner a second chance.*

Shortly after Barry's arrest, one of Washington, D.C.'s leading pastors visited Marion Barry in his jail cell. The pastor decided to champion Barry's case. Public repentance preceded a revival-like campaign. Barry's comeback campaign emphasized his religious conversion and personal renewal. The citizens of our nation's capital forgave Barry and allowed him to return to office, demonstrating a depth of grace and compassion that bewildered most of the country's citizens.

Many whites look at Barry's miraculous escape from major criminal charges and his return to political office as evidence of the low ethical standards among leaders in the black community. Giving such a "reprehensible character" a second chance seems to be a moral anomaly or gross hypocrisy. A number of church leaders have even bemoaned the situation, expressing their concern that we might be dispensing personal grace to the point of corporate disgrace.

But there is a totally different perspective one might take on this situation. The black church places an extraordinarily high value on giving even the worst sinner a second chance. This is not seen as permissiveness but as an attempt to avoid a caustic, judgmental or holier-than-thou attitude. From this vantage point, every individual must be honored and valued. The essence of participating in a community of faith is to experience the full-orbed love that enables a person to grow and develop. As the apostle Paul stated, "God's kindness leads you toward repentance" (Rom. 2:4). God's goodness can be communicated to wounded seekers through acceptance and forgiveness. This is a philosophy of inclusion, which serves as the bedrock of the relational dynamic of the African-American church.

In response, one might ask three questions: Is this relational philosophy biblical? What are the historic factors that brought the black church to this place? How has this attitude of inclusion positively impacted the lives of black Christians?

RELATIONAL PHILOSOPHY

The Old Testament has been given to the Church partly to demonstrate many truths that are revealed or explained more fully in the New Testament. The old adage states that the New Testament is in the Old concealed and that the Old Testament is in the New revealed. In keeping with this adage, the black church has decided to serve as the community's "city of refuge" (Num. 35:25-26,28,32), a concept drawn from the Old Testament. During the time of Joshua, designated cities were set aside as the modern-day equivalent of safe houses. These isolated but secure zones were designed for people who had accidentally committed murder. Guilty parties could run to these cities and apply for asylum. Men and women would be required to appear before the elders of the city, offering their testimony for consideration. If these elders were convinced of the accidental nature of the death and the desire of the perpetrator to clean up his life, they would grant asylum to the person in question.

How does this "city of refuge" concept play out in twenty-first-century American life? In our society, there are many people who feel as though they have committed the unpardonable sin. Whether the sin is abortion, divorce, homosexuality or drug addiction, some churches have reduced these people to social pariahs or lepers. Such reactions are why millions of Americans perceive the Christian Church to be a place of judgment more than a place of spiritual advocacy or refuge.

HISTORICAL FACTORS

The black church in this country has been a haven of acceptance for people from all walks of life. The emphasis on repentance and restoration, with subsequent acceptance by a community of fellow pardoned sinners, has been a common thread that has connected rich and poor, young and old, educated and illiterate.

The relational strength of black churches most likely has its roots in the African tribal system. The traditional African believes that his or her connection with a community is essential to his or her personal identity and survival. In South Africa, the Khosa tribe has a word that they use for community, *ubuntu*. This word speaks of covenant commitment.

In a world defined by ubuntu, the individual pursues corporate goals more passionately than personal goals. There is a sense that the individual owes a debt to the group. In extreme cases, community members hide their friends from police or other legitimate authorities, thus risking their personal reputation.

These ubuntu values are apparent in today's black church.

In fact, black-church analysts use concepts and terminology similar to "ubuntu" to describe the current relational atmosphere of the churches they study. Carlyle Stewart stated:

> Relational norms of the black culture include the following: valuing and respecting others as persons; developing relationships of mutual concern and trust; caring for and responding to the needs of the family; extended family, and community; raising and caring for elders, children, and adults; respecting eminent domain of matriarchal and patriarchal authority; reverence for God.[1]

There are many aspects of American history that reinforce the need for black solidarity. Slavery challenged many of the tribal and national bonds between the sons and daughters of Africa who took up residence on American soil. Nothing unites a people as much as the presence of a common foe. Obviously, the struggle for social and political freedom for blacks continues to this day. During the post-Civil War days, the black church's care lovingly helped give birth to a free community that enjoyed a sense of relational security and economic stability.

As the 1800s came to a close, the agricultural base of the American economy began to shift. Industrialization led blacks to migrate to urban centers. They migrated first to southern cities before filtering up to the metropolitan areas of the Northeast. No longer exclusively tied to farming and related endeavors, blacks reestablished their lives around communities of faith. Churches became the channel through which they were helped during the tough financial times and through which they developed a network of sustaining relationships.

By the start of the twentieth century, more than half of the

7 million African-Americans over the age of 10 belonged to a Christian church.[2] Clearly the "city of refuge" has demonstrated its ability to adapt to the needs of the black community.

INCLUSIVE ATTITUDE

Like many effective strategies in the business world, trial and error has produced approaches that really work. Armed with few viable choices, black leaders strategically developed a culturally accepted worldview and used it as a bridge to build a structure pleasing to God. The city of refuge or ubuntu paradigm takes the notion of the church as a loving family to another level. The feeling of connection that members experience gets directed into three progressive, interrelated steps: placement, purpose and passion.

Placement

If a person truly begins to identify with a spiritual community, the desire to help or support it becomes a natural outgrowth of that connection. If unintimidating service opportunities or needs are presented, a newcomer can rapidly transition from spectator to participant with very little effort. That shift ushers in dramatic changes in identity and spiritual maturity. Curiously, this personal epiphany is sometimes aided by a church's establishing relatively low barriers to membership. For many blacks, the simple offer of unconditional acceptance eases them into a more intense commitment to both Christ and the church community.

Indisputably, black churches have historically aimed at lay mobilization as a key to growth and impact. Because black churches did not have either the funds or the pool of theologically trained leaders from which to draw, these motivated, nonpaid "ministers" were relied on to be the church rather than simply to come to the church and watch the paid professionals do the work. In His sovereign wisdom, God led black churches to a ministry model in which lay people enabled the church to be effective while also developing a deep reservoir of personal relationships based upon a common commitment to faith in action.

Floyd Massey and Samuel Berry McKinney have done a masterful job of sharing insights into the inner workings of the black church:

> Large numbers of people are involved in the worship experience of black churches. Gigantic usher boards execute their responsibilities, in some instances, with the precision of the changing of the guard at Buckingham Palace, London, England; numerous vested choirs for all age groups sing every Sunday; large deacons' boards, arrayed in black suits and white gloves, plus deaconesses'/mothers' boards, bedecked in white dresses on Communion Sunday, are part of the Sunday drama in most urban black churches throughout the nation. Participation in the life of their church affirms and sustains the sense of "somebodiness" so greatly needed by people victimized by a racist society six days a week.[3]

Internal ministry placement is enhanced by the high honor paid to church volunteers. Honor is conferred differently across cultures but the principle of honor is transferable to every ethnic group. The development of multiple boards and committees gives significant entry points for motivated members to serve, without compromising the primary leadership authority within the church. Further, the prolific use of titles confers a sense of significance upon these active individuals. All of these methods allow lay members to develop a sense of ownership of their church and its activities. Such ownership is the first step toward aligning with corporate purpose, which may result in a passion for spiritual things as the final goal.

Purpose

God created us to be in relationship with Himself and with other people. Highly effective churches have tapped into this inclination by intentionally addressing every person's need to belong to something special. A church that fosters true community is indeed something special. Our study of the black church suggests that transformation-focused small groups are central to the health of high-impact African-American churches. The research reveals that in general, black churches have a higher percentage of congregants involved in small groups, that a higher proportion of black adults participate in small groups and that the high-impact churches register the highest percentage of adult small-group participation of any churches.

In the evangelical church at large, small groups often stand alone as distinct ministry initiatives designed to promote relationships and discipleship. Some ministry professionals criticize the idea that task-oriented groups can produce lasting, cohesive relationships that move members to spiritual maturity. The experience of high-impact black churches shows that supporting a highly divergent assortment of relational groups (e.g., Sunday School classes, auxiliaries, discipleship groups and service ministry teams) makes a major difference in the lives of members by adding purpose to their church connection. Placement and purpose in an atmosphere of acceptance often yield passion.

Passion

Believers who possess a viable role within a community of faith and have a clear sense of purpose typically devote themselves to maximizing their investment in God's kingdom. Through the encouragement that they receive from relationships with like-minded disciples, their enthusiasm pushes them to persevere

Placement and purpose in an atmosphere of acceptance often yield passion.

and to achieve more than might have been expected of them. Further, the accountability they experience through trusting relationships fosters continued development of skills and maturity.

Taken together, these relationships help individual followers of Christ achieve impact and transformation that never would have occurred had they pursued their faith in isolation. Consequently, there is a flowing passion about Christ, ministry for Christ and the value of the church that would not have emerged otherwise. And it is that passion that fuels continued influence for the Kingdom.

One of the clear outgrowths of the relational value received is the heightened level of spiritual pursuit evident in the lives of black people. As noted earlier in this book, blacks have substantially higher levels of faith involvement—Bible reading, prayer, small-group attendance, fasting and Sunday School participation—than any other ethnic group in the nation. And these levels of activity are even higher in the most effective black churches.

LASTING RELATIONSHIPS

The person-to-person connections facilitated in high-impact churches become the fuel that propels otherwise lethargic, distracted and alienated individuals into people flush with excitement and hope. It all starts with a determination by church leaders to invite people into a genuine family in which love freely flows and is advanced by an environment in which each individual sees the benefits of connecting with others on the same journey of significance.

Don't miss the fact that relationships do not just happen. High-impact churches are very intentional when it comes to creating opportunities, building bridges, fostering connections and reinforcing the bonds that have been established. More than a few of the pastors of these churches informed us that one of the most debilitating assumptions a church can own is that people know how to develop lasting friendships and that, given the chance to do so, they will aggressively pursue such friendships. In postmodern America, people are hungry for relationships but virtually paralyzed when it comes time to forge them.

It is also worth noting that a number of the great churches we have studied prioritize how they invest their relational resources. In those congregations, the bulk of the relationship-oriented resources are committed to building strong ties among congregants. A lesser amount is devoted to relationships with people outside the church. However, there is a clear expectation—one that is stated and modeled—that a portion of members' relational capacity will be devoted to non-Christians, with the hope of eventually connecting those individuals to Christ.

But unless believers are well connected within their church and feel emotionally secure among their tribe, the chances of them inviting others to join the tribe are slim.

Making a concerted effort to help people connect with God and with other people is a crucial factor in the health and growth of a high-impact church. The return on this investment is massive but must be intelligently conceived and pursued.

CHAPTER 10

NEW HORIZONS TO PURSUE

Human progress never rolls in on wheels of inevitability. It comes
through the tireless efforts and persistent work of men willing to be
coworkers with God, and without this hard work, time itself becomes
an ally of the forces of social stagnation.

—MARTIN LUTHER KING, JR.

The research among blacks and their churches has both confirmed and revealed important aspects of contemporary ministry.
As a result of our being practitioners of the art of ministry, the
insights gleaned from this process have challenged our understanding of transformative ministry and disturbed our sense of
comfort as leaders. How good it is to be shaken up by fresh
insights captured through the experience of other practitioners!

We hope you have been "keeping score" as you've read this
book—that is, you have attempted to capture every transferable
concept that might add value to your ministry and its efforts to
advance the kingdom of God. Given the breadth of the descriptions covered in these chapters, it is possible that you may have

missed a few insights or perhaps your experience has lent a point of view different from ours. With that in mind, let us close this volume with a few additional observations that might spark further reflection and examination.

GROWING A HEALTHY CULTURE

Every church develops its own internal culture. Because culture encompasses many divergent elements—values, symbols, language, customs, rules and so forth—no two churches possess an identical culture. However, the experience of high-impact churches reinforces the importance of intentionally engineering and monitoring a church's culture so as to foster healthy ministry and consistent life transformation.

One of the most compelling observations is the value of creating a culture of grace. It seems that black people are able to give grace to others, and thus generate a welcoming and vibrant ministry environment, because they have received God's grace and recognize the astounding gift that it is. The grace received by African-Americans is no different, qualitatively, from the grace received by other Americans. However, the reaction of blacks to that gift from God is unique. And it is their realization of the miracle of that gift that seems to be responsible for blacks' ability to forgive and accept fellow sinners into the fold readily and easily. *What would happen if all of our country's churches had a grace-permeated and grace-giving culture—not as an afterthought but as a fundamental building block of the ministry?*

Another aspect of the vitality of the culture in high-impact churches is their willingness to partner with anyone who is committed to the same outcomes. These churches labor alongside large churches and small churches, government agencies and nonreligious nonprofit organizations, white community groups, black neighborhood groups and Hispanic associations. These churches are realistic about their ministry: They know that if they wait until they have total control, they will never get out of the starting block. They realize that if they have to raise all the money and develop all the talent to complete the jobs before them, they will be left with a series of half-completed ministry efforts—and a long line of shattered or disappointed lives. *What would happen if every church saw itself as inadequate to complete the vision it pursues and therefore dedicated itself to teaming up with whomever they could enlist as partners in that pursuit?*

MAKING A MINISTRY IMPACT

The quality of leadership provided to a church is perhaps the single most significant factor in its ability to become a high-impact ministry. This element transcends the effects of race, geography, economics, size and physical plant. Without fail, we found a strong correlation between ministry impact and the leadership capacity of the pastor, staff and laity.

One of the brilliant tactics of the churches we have examined is their assignment of roles and titles to laypeople. Leaders generally have more opportunities to use their gifts than they can satisfy, effectively placing church in competition with other institutions for the commitment of the individual. As much as we might like to behave altruistically and believe that the opportunity to serve God through the church is so special that it operates above such worldly contrivances as titles and other perks, the reality is that people respond to such matters. Black churches are not trying to flatter people by offering such things; it is just one more way of communicating the value of individuals to the ministry and rewarding them for making a good decision. *How would the typical American church benefit from "deputizing" all the gifted leaders who are associated with the church by blessing them with every available resource and perk and turning them loose to do what God brought them to that church to accomplish?*

One of the most astonishing revelations has been the influence of the pastors in black churches. It is not because of their force of personality but because they knowingly embrace the role of spokesperson for the black community. What is so intriguing is that this role is available to every pastor, regardless

Why don't more church leaders translate their in-church authority to outside-of-church influence?

of the congregation's dominant ethnicity or the socioeconomic character of the church, yet only black pastors automatically embrace this function. This thread of responsibility—intentionally developing and using their influence for moral, spiritual, familial, political and economic purposes—inarguably fosters the ability to introduce faith principles into every domain of life and culture.

The results of this determination to be a player are really quite stunning. As we examine the place of the Church in communities, we generally find that the pastors of high-impact black churches are widely known and are respected as leaders by their peers in government, business and the nonprofit sector. They can open doors, initiate debates, plant ideas, access resources and build bridges where other religious leaders are not even welcome. If the culture wars are a serious battlefront for the

Church, high-impact black pastors have already established themselves as strategic warriors in that challenge. *Why don't more church leaders translate their in-church authority to outside-of-church influence? How would America change if more of its spiritual leaders reenvisioned their role and applied their God-given authority to every dimension of life?*

MAINTAINING A CHRISTLIKE ATTITUDE

Even if you are an outsider unfamiliar with the typical perspectives and behaviors of black Christians and their churches, you cannot help but be struck by the power of attitude. The self-image and sense of heritage incorporated in the faith of African-Americans is a major influence on who they are as believers and on how they serve God. Certainly these followers of Christ take many things for granted in their lives—we all do—but fortunately, their identity in Christ is not one of them. There are likely ways of integrating such matters more fruitfully in the lives of other believers as well. *What difference would it make for white Christians in this nation to understand the sacrifices that have been made by their ancestors so that they not only can worship freely but also are able to lead a bold Christian life in every dimension of their existence?*

In specific terms, it has been startling to observe how bold many black people are in sharing their faith in Christ with fellow blacks who are outside the fold. Why are they so willing to speak in unambiguous ways about their faith? It seems to relate intimately to how real their salvation has become for them. The tangibility of their salvation may be attributed to a variety of components: preaching that constantly reaffirms their eternal security and its value, the connection between being heaven-bound and the hope that this provides for the challenges faced on Earth, a sense that with Christ on their side they can never lose a battle, the feeling of personal obligation to other members of an oppressed people group and so forth. The point is that most blacks have not succumbed to the cultural pressure simply to take God's grace as another deserved benefit of living in America and reducing that forgiveness to mere "cheap grace" (i.e., when we pray the "sinner's prayer," God automatically dispenses eternal security and we both get on with life without having to worry any further about the matter). Perhaps because they see so little hope for themselves on Earth, most blacks treat their salvation as a genuine and unparalleled gift from God. *If other churches were able to make God's gift of salvation something so remarkable and so breathtaking that every believer was forced to stop regularly to give God renewed appreciation and to be reminded continually that being bought with the blood of Christ was for a Kingdom purpose, how would this world be altered?*

So many churches in the United States have embraced the philosophy du jour, which is to set short-term goals and work hard to accomplish those outcomes in the belief that their cumulative effect will produce major change and positive societal benefits. The problem with this perspective is that it is generally disconnected from God's vision, which is always long-term in nature. In fact, God's vision usually outlives the visionary to whom that portrait of a preferable future was initially delivered.

High-impact black churches are tethered to a long-term vision of transformation that anchors their behavior in unique ways. They have persisted in the face of persecution, economic challenges and political opposition because of their insistence on staying true to God's ultimate call upon their ministry. Rather than settle for a small gain here and a compromised victory there, these churches keep their eyes fixed on the larger prize they have been called to pursue—whatever it may be— and doggedly pursue that outcome. *How would America itself be transformed if every church understood its unique vision from God and refused to rest until it had faithfully fulfilled its calling to bring that heaven-sent vision to reality?*

FOCUSING ON TRANSFORMED LIVES

Some ministry colleagues have listened to our excitement about the great African-American churches we have been privileged to study and then tried to dampen that enthusiasm by reminding us that there are no perfect churches. As long as people (aka sinners) are involved, it is true that every church will have its flaws. And as our well-meaning friends like to point out, even the greatest churches fail to produce perfect people. Once again, we acknowledge that we have been confronted with a truism.

But our excitement over the possibilities of what a human-laden church can become remains undampened! One of the most striking realizations we arrived at during this research is that many of the greatest black churches in the nation are virtually unknown—sometimes even within the black community itself! Several of these ministries draw more than 20,000 people every single weekend to their campuses, yet there are no stories about them in *USA Today*, their pastors are not invited to the White House, bookstores do not stock how-to books and curriculum emanating from their churches, and they don't run nationally known ministry conferences with satellite feeds to remote locations. And, we discovered, they don't care about the lack of public notice and professional adulation. Why? Their focus is on the transformation happening in the lives of their people and in the communities in which they reside. They run the race to win the prize but the prize is nothing less than renewed minds and hearts that lead to transformed lives. *Have we made ministry too much of an industry and thus lost sight of our first love? Have we created a parallel universe of ministry icons and celebrities but missed the very purpose of our calling? What would the United States look like if "successful" churches spent less time posing and positioning for widespread influence in the ministry world and instead applied those resources to the family, economic, political and cultural challenges resident in their communities?*

ESTABLISHING THE RIGHT PRIORITIES

It is always impressive when you observe a job well done. Watching high-impact black churches in action has reminded us that establishing and maintaining appropriate priorities are always critical elements to success. So it has been a joy to see African-Americans joined together in unrestrained worship, seeing that these churches are less worried about taking care of business on Sunday mornings than they are about fostering the opportunity for a supernatural connection to be made between forgiven sinners and a holy God. It has been comforting to watch as these churches have continued to do the monotonous heavy-lifting of reforming the minds and hearts of wayward people so that they might become true disciples of Jesus Christ. It has been refreshing to behold churches that emphasize the centrality of significant relationships among people who have only one thing in common: an unquenchable thirst to know and be known by God. And what a challenge it is to be in the presence of people who have so deeply embraced the idea that "faith without works is dead" (Jas. 2:26, *KJV*) that there is no discussion about the principle itself, only about the most appropriate way to carry it out.

High-impact churches—whether they minister to whites, blacks, Hispanics, Asians, Native Americans or multiethnic congregations—develop good habits in their people. These ministries know what matters and put their resources into the right priorities. By identifying the pillars of Christian ministry— worship, evangelism, discipleship, community service, steward- ship, accountable relationships—and supporting meaningful ministry in those areas with courageous, visionary leadership and ways of building and reinforcing strong families, these churches change the world. *How would our world be changed if every church cleared its radar screen of distractions and focused on doing what is most important?*

You are made in the image of God, for the purposes of God; and you live in order to love, obey and serve God.

SETTING A GODLY STANDARD

Sometimes we hear at conferences that ministries such as the high-impact churches we have explored have set the standard high for other churches. Nothing could be farther from the truth. It is God who sets the standards for us. The more we stop competing with other churches and focus instead on His vision and calling for each of us, the more likely we are to become the Church He wants us to be.

So what, then, is the value of having gleaned so much infor- mation about what high-impact churches do? Perhaps as much as anything it is to realize and recognize the unlimited possi- bilities and potential resident within every church and every follower of Christ. Your church can go places it hasn't even dreamed of reaching! As a leader, you have been created by God to direct His people to victory! As a disciple, you have been given power and authority that you could never exhaust in a lifetime of heroic effort!

These truths become abundantly real as you watch small congregations of people who have little standing in the economic world change their part of the universe, bit by bit and day by day. This perspective takes on greater meaning as you study an unschooled pastor who effectively introduces new ideas and old-world values into a hip-hop age. You cannot help but be moved when you see a committed believer stand up for what is right despite overwhelming odds of failure—and prevail, not because of cleverly orchestrated politics or astounding articulation but because of faithfulness to truth.

The story of black churches is based on the notion of never forgetting where you came from and why you exist. You are made in the image of God, for the purposes of God; and you live in order to love, obey and serve God. Rest assured that you are not alone in that condition. We have seen the tireless, joy-filled ministry of millions of others who share that same mantle of godly authority and purpose and have invested themselves in rising to the title of "good and faithful servant" (Matt. 25:21,23). May you join them in pursuit of the only genuine meaning that can be known in this life: becoming a high-impact player for God and His kingdom.

CHURCH PORTRAITS

LEADERSHIP

BETHEL AME CHURCH
BALTIMORE, MARYLAND

In 1784, a small group of free black men and women began a prayer group. Their vision was to establish a church that was open to people of color. Like Jacob of the Old Testament, who found a place of spiritual refuge that he named Bethel (see Gen. 35:15), these early leaders did the same. They made a covenant with God that He would protect and prosper them at this place in Baltimore that they called Bethel. As the church grew, it became involved in ministry to blacks across the city and all over the world.

THE PASTOR

As senior pastor, Rev. Dr. Frank Madison Reid III has excelled at piloting one of his denomination's oldest congregations as it has moved into a vibrant twenty-first-century stream of faith.

Reid received his undergraduate degree from Yale University, a M.Div. from Harvard Divinity School and a Doctor of Ministry degree as a Samuel Proctor Fellow from the United Theological Seminary.

All of this education has not kept Reid from effectively crossing age, gender and social boundaries. In fact, under his leadership, Bethel has seen more than 20,000 conversions since 1988. In addition to the many converts, the church has also had a tremendous impact on the quality of life in Baltimore. Dr. Reid is the author of *The Nehemiah Plan: Preparing the Church to Rebuild Broken Lives* and *Restoring the House of God.* Prior to pastoring at Bethel, Dr. Reid led a thriving congregation (Ward AME) in Los Angeles, California. In that setting, he developed several ministry models for effectively reaching African-American men.

HISTORY

In 1811, the church sent missionaries to Africa to establish a Christian colony. This outreach eventually became part of the nation of Liberia. In 1816, Bethel helped give birth to the African Methodist Episcopal (AME) denomination. This involvement began a long tradition of pastoral leaders from Bethel, who affected the AME denomination, the church in America and missionary activities abroad. As the years went on, Bethel pastors grew in stature and influence. By the 1850s, Bethel had grown to a membership of 1,500. As a result of its numeric strength, Bethel AME Church became the center of the black struggle for equality. Abolitionists and other Christian activists frequently spoke from this historic pulpit.

One of Bethel's greatest pastors was Bishop Daniel Payne.

Becoming pastor in 1874, Payne directed schools for children in Baltimore and stressed the need for an educated ministry. He developed a systematic program of studies for ministerial education for the entire AME Church. Later, Bishop Payne became the president of Wilberforce University.

Bethel has been quite active in church planting during its 220-year history, giving birth to most of the AME churches in Maryland. Bethel has continued to be a center of the black struggle for equality. In addition to its regular church services, Bethel has been a favorite community convening point used for meetings to discuss the political issues affecting the entire black community. As a result of such meetings, many groundbreaking trends were set. Bethel member Violet Hill Whyte became the first black police officer in Baltimore as a result of Bethel's influence. Local pastors rallied Baltimore's black community from the church's sanctuary to support the efforts of Martin Luther King, Jr. Even marches protesting apartheid in South Africa were organized within the Bethel's walls.

Currently, Pastor Reid is leading a building campaign to acquire 256 acres of land for an expansion site in western Baltimore County, where 50 percent of its members reside. The church's television program, *The Outreach of Love*, can be seen in 123 countries. There are 14,500 persons who are on the membership rolls at Bethel, with more than 4,000 people in attendance at weekend services. Currently, there are more than 40 active and thriving ministries. These ministries include the Bethel Outreach Center, Bethel Christian School, Saturday Day School, the AIDS ministry, the Freedom Now ministry (which works with recovering substance abusers), the prison ministry, the Hands of Glory ministry (for the hearing-impaired) and the media outreach.

LEADERSHIP

Historically, Bethel AME has attracted strong leaders. Both the style and the content of its leadership teams have varied widely from generation to generation. Many of its pastors were forerunners, both in Baltimore and in the African-American church nationally.

Reid has developed an effective leadership team that meets the church's current needs. One church leader describes him as "a futurist who can simultaneously work on external expansion and deep personal development of leaders." Reid's philosophy has been that the senior leader should spend time with his leaders, instilling the vision of the church and creating a unique church culture that propels it toward its vision. Bethel does this in several ways: monthly leadership meetings, roundtable accountability meetings with senior leaders in which they discuss their own personal growth and the assignment of senior leaders to disciple one or more junior leaders. All leaders at Bethel are expected to grow, to be examples before the congregation and to mentor others. Reid models personal growth by reading three to six books a week, in addition to giving systematic attention to the Scriptures. Despite his personal thirst for knowledge, Reid knows that character will determine the true strength of his leadership team. With this in mind, he challenges his trustees, stewards and ministry heads to be true servants. These officers may have the ability to delegate to many employees at their place of work, yet in the church a different approach is needed. They may need to pick up litter from the floor after a church event in order to model a hands-on commitment to service.

Reid's collaborative leadership style gives maximum opportunity of expression for department leaders, while maintaining a clear strategic thrust for the overall church. In addition to this strength, the leaders we interviewed cited four components of Bethel's leadership development program that have impacted them the most.

1. **Training and equipping.** Bethel's training is multifaceted. It includes character development, leadership skills, business approaches, personal development and spiritual enlightenment. The church avoids creating a cliquish leadership bottleneck by making leadership training available to anyone who wants it. When a training session is scheduled, anyone who wants to attend is welcome. Reid sets a theme and strategic direction for both the church worship services and the leadership-training curriculum each year. Each December, Pastor Reid hosts an all-day leadership summit designed to prepare the team for the year ahead. He has had nationally known speakers, Harvard University professors and seasoned business leaders address his team. For the remainder of the year, he personally trains the leaders and carefully selects outside speakers that will supplement his work.

2. **Correct placement.** Bethel is determined to give its leaders assignments in which they can be fruitful. Ministry assignments are reconsidered annually. This allows people to develop their ministry effectiveness on a fast track, with the utmost accountability. If the placement of particular leaders is not working out, they can be removed at the end of one year without losing face. Furthermore,

limiting assignments to one year affords the ability to reassign leaders as necessary due to misplacement or to new opportunities without the challenge of territorialism.

3. **Life accountability.** Bethel works hard at creating a sense of camaraderie among its key leaders. Reid's strong emphasis on personal growth challenges most volunteers to give their best in terms of time, energy and faithfulness. He takes personal interest in the private lives of those who serve the church. Reid is not afraid to confront those who have major issues of character or moral sin. Yet these kinds of confrontations are handled in a caring, loving way.

4. **Spiritual and skill mentoring.** In each board, Bethel utilizes the maximum number of people allowed by the AME Church. Reid does this to involve more people in ministry leadership. If there is a Steward Board, he creates a junior steward board. There he places younger, less experienced people to learn from those who have had more time in church leadership. Reid also pairs people up with these duplicate boards. The senior people are assigned to the juniors in order to allow the younger ones to have an effect on the church programs and policy. It also teaches the junior members principles for their future leadership assignments. Leadership should be a transferable commodity to the next generation. There is a mutual exchange of the historic roots of the ministry with the new ideas of younger members. Bethel's long history of effective leadership has been

built entirely on bringing others along to learn the business of ministry and to grow in their spiritual walk. The training of leaders needs to include skill building, character development, business principles and spiritual enrichment.

In addition to witnessing the four strengths listed above, anyone visiting Bethel will note the high number of men in the congregation and in leadership roles. Men make up 40 percent of Bethel membership compared to 20 percent to 25 percent of churches in similar communities. Early in Reid's ministry he discovered a way to attract black men and prepare them for leadership. Many things were involved in creating an atmosphere in which black men are nurtured. First, Reid developed male leaders by creating a men's-only Bible study. This ministry was aimed at building the self-esteem and ministry confidence of the men who attended the church. Second, Reid created a men's security ministry called the Mighty Men of God. This ministry encouraged male teamwork and camaraderie, which helped men gain a sense of acceptance and belonging. While this was being done, Reid continued to raise up strong female leaders as well. He does not believe that men have to be developed at the expense of women but believes that both genders should be equipped to take their unique places in the church.

You can find out more about Bethel AME Church at www.bethel1.org.

DISCIPLESHIP

OAK CLIFF BIBLE FELLOWSHIP
DALLAS, TEXAS

In early 1976, two regional leaders, Reuben Connor and Gene Getz, felt that a strong Bible church was needed in the Oak Cliff area. Oak Cliff had been known for its churches in the past decades. So many churches had grown up on Tenth Street that it was dubbed "The Street of Churches" in *Ripley's Believe It or Not*. Although this region had historically been all white, in the 1960s a large number of blacks moved to the neighborhood. The existing churches did not seem to be reaching African-Americans or meeting the contemporary needs of the community. Connor and Getz desired a church that would provide an alternative Christian experience amidst strong Bible teaching.

THE PASTOR

Dr. Anthony Evans is cofounder and senior pastor of Oak Cliff Bible Fellowship (OCBF). Dr. Evans was the first African-American to graduate with a doctoral degree from Dallas Theological Seminary. Prior to studying in Dallas, he graduated from both Carver Bible College and Dallas Theological Seminary with academic honors. Dr. Evans was one of the first African-Americans to lay out a strategic plan to impact an entire city. He is a speaker at Promise Keepers' assemblies and is featured in crusades and Bible conferences in the United States and overseas. The recipient of many awards, Dr. Evans has received an honorary doctorate of Humane Letters from Eastern College in Pennsylvania. Further, he and his Family Research Center received the Marian Pfister Anschutz Award in recognition of his "dedication to protecting, encouraging and strengthening the American family." In addition, Outstanding Young Men of America named Dr. Evans "Father of the Year" in 1989. Dr. Evans serves on the Board of Incorporate Members for Dallas Theological Seminary as well as on the boards of the National Religious Broadcasters and the Urban Evangelical Mission.

Dr. Evans is also a prolific writer with numerous books to his credit including *God Is More Than Enough*; *Life Essentials: For Knowing God Better, Experiencing God Deeper, Loving God More*; *Tony Evans Speaks Out on Being Single and Satisfied*; and *The Battle Is the Lord's*. His books are filled with penetrating scriptural insights and much practical wisdom. Most people would be pleased being an award-winning pastor and author. Dr. Evans is tireless in his desire to reach the world. His third major role is founder and president of the Urban Alternative. This national organization seeks to bring about spiritual renewal in urban America through the church. The radio broadcast sponsored by this ministry is aired by over 500 stations daily in the United States and penetrates over 40 countries.

A SOLID ALTERNATIVE

The name "Urban Alternative" comes from a vision deep within Dr. Evans's heart. Just as Joshua challenged the children of Israel to choose whom they would serve (see Josh. 24:15), Dr. Evans has long sought to present to the world a Christian alternative to their lives. He has carried this message and spiritual perspective to the world as both an evangelist and a pastor. Therefore, when Dr. Reuben Connor and Dr. Gene Getz asked Evans to consider pastoring a Christ-centered, Bible-based church, it seemed like a natural fit. Evans accepted and invited Rev. Crawford Loritts, formerly of Here's Life America, to help initiate this work with 10 members.

Only a month after its inception, the church began the Learning Center, which provides biblical teaching designed specifically for children. The church grew rapidly, and Pastor Evans realized that he needed help in overseeing the spiritual development of the congregation. Martin Hawkins, also a graduate of Dallas Theological Seminary, was hired as the church's assistant pastor.

In the mid-1980s, the church added the Alternative Community Development Services to further adult education and involvement with the community. Vacation Bible School was expanded to include the entire family. As part of the alternative vision to provide a biblical foundation for all aspects of life, a Christian school (now called Fellowship Christian Academy) was established.

In 1988, the church opened its newly built Family Life Center that featured a resource center and bookstore to provide Christian materials for continued spiritual development. Over the next few years, ministry in the Village Oaks Apartment complex was started, which included weekly Bible studies for adults, youth and children.

By the middle of the 1990s, a large percentage of the congregation had completed the core curriculum of the Center for Christian Growth. The gender-based discipleship program M'PACT (Mentoring People According to Christ's Teaching) was designed to help believers mature by meeting their spiritual and emotional needs.

As of 2004, Oak Cliff Bible Fellowship has nearly 6,000 members. It has endeavored to exemplify God's alternative lifestyle for over 20 years. The church motto is "Discipling the

Church to Impact the World." The church members of Oak Cliff attempt to demonstrate actively Christ's teaching in their respective areas of influence.

THE PRACTICE OF DISCIPLESHIP

Pastor Martin Hawkins has been a member of the church since its beginning and part of the pastoral staff for more than 25 years. He has served in almost every aspect of ministry at Oak Cliff, including preaching, leadership training and development, counseling and teaching. He has been instrumental in much of the curriculum development in the discipleship-training programs at Oak Cliff.

The multifaceted discipleship program at OCBF includes a Bible college, a Bible institute, a strong Christian education department, children and youth ministries and a self-study course for personal maturity.

The Christian education department purpose is to promote learning among God's people but goes further to produce a response of personal obedience to the Scriptures. They utilize six strategies: (1) teaching the Word of God, (2) modeling the Word of God, (3) edifying in the Word of God, (4) maturing in the Word of God, (5) equipping with the Word of God and (6) fellowshiping based on the Word of God. From these strategies alone, it is easy to see that learning the Word is only the first step of the Oak Cliff's discipleship process. The church expects high results from its programs and believes that its success in discipling others is demonstrated by the changed lives of the people who have learned the Word of God at Oak Cliff.

Dr. Hawkins sets forth six recommendations for people attempting to build a strong discipleship program:

1. **Create a process for personal accountability**. OCBF has developed a biblical model for church discipline along with biblical conflict-resolution models.

2. **Develop a core curriculum**. At the core of this recommendation is the need for every church to develop its own clearly articulated discipleship strategy. OCBF's Bible Institute is based on the belief that purpose-driven living begins with purpose-driven preparation. The institute provides foundational teachings in order to live a well-grounded Christian life, as well as courses that will build skills toward career success. The two core curriculum courses are Principles for Leaders and Practices of Leadership. OCBF's Bible Institute schedules a variety of classes that build toward certification in chosen areas. The uniqueness of this institute is that it takes into consideration the lifestyles of twenty-first-century Christians. Most of the core curriculum courses and specialty tracks comprise four sessions that culminate in a practicum. The practicum is a supervised application of the ministry theory that has been taught. Students are assigned a mentor who guides them in their experience.

3. **Pass on passion, not just information.** Churches need to consider the influence their current training has on the lives of their students, not merely the amount of knowledge that the students will possess. An evaluation process would be prudent in order to assess the curriculum chosen, the teachers or trainers

selected and the style of lessons that the church has provided in regard to the difference made in the total discipleship of the individuals taking the class.

4. **Make class times convenient.** Churches should consider the lifestyles of their students and their time limitations. A hallmark of Oak Cliff is the flexibility to structure the schedule to serve its people. Commute time, family responsibilities and job-related demands compete for whatever free time congregants have. Keeping these in mind will afford the opportunity for more participants and therefore more success. For example, a church might offer classes for youth, children and adults simultaneously and provide child care for infants. The number of class sessions, the day of the week and the time of day that classes are held can promote or diminish class size. Some of OCBF's classes are offered as seminars—students are required to read and prepare for a daylong intensive session held on Saturday.

5. **Create a self-study track.** Churches need to help their parishioners continue their growth in Christ. Instead of creating all of the materials, the senior pastor could compile a recommended reading list each year. This would amplify his annual sermon topics or convey his desires for specific aspects of growth among members.

6. **Offer life-skills training.** Consideration should be given to the idea of skill-based training within the church environment. Churches might survey their

congregations for teachers or trainers by occupation and by gift for specific areas of career development or motivation. This not only could open the opportunity to increase the capacity of church members for success in the marketplace but also could be used as a vehicle for reaching the greater community.

The Discipline Process

These procedures are based on the spiritual principles given to us by the Lord Jesus Christ in Matthew 18:15-20. Church discipline is an indication of a church's love for both Christ and its local members. Church leaders should view themselves as functioning in a parental role that has been assigned to them by the Lord through the mandate of Scripture. OCBF's discipline process is as follows:

Step 1: Discipline begins with any concerned Christian brother or sister who becomes aware of an offense in a fellow believer's life. This concerned person does not have to be a pastor or ordained leader. First of all, the concerned person goes to the other, one-on-one, person-to-person, friend-to-friend, and in love encourages him or her to repent—to turn from the sin, or error, and put a halt to it (see v. 15).

This is to be kept between the concerned person and the person in error. The moment someone else is told, it becomes gossip. What if what the person thinks he or she has seen is not true and yet someone else has been told? False gossip about someone has just been spread all over the church. *Above all else, this matter is to be kept private.*

Step 2: What if the sinning believer refuses to listen and will not repent? This is where Galatians 6:1 kicks in: Some spiritual person needs to go with the concerned individual—one or two people who are close to the situation, a ministry head, deacon or deaconess, elder or pastoral staff (see Matt. 18:16)

Step 3: If step 2 does not work, then the whole church (unfortunately) becomes involved (see v. 17).

Even though this is the last step, this is where the work begins because the sin demands restoration. When the sin was private, private confession and repentance were in order; but when the sin becomes public, public confession and repentance are the order of the day.

- A letter (sent by registered mail) from the church and a phone call from a designated leader, exhorting the erring member to come to his or her senses, are made.
- One month later, the erring member is warned that his or her sin will be brought publicly before the congregation. If this person responds positively, the public announcement will be canceled. If the person does not respond positively, the process will continue with removal from all ministry responsibilities.
- If there is no positive response over the next 30 days, another registered letter will be sent. In the letter, the person will be informed that he or she will be excommunicated from the church in 30 days (the date being specified), that he or she can still avoid this action by dealing with the rebellion and that the church stands ready and willing to assist him or her.
- If there is no positive response from the second registered letter, the following three things will recur: (1) the person's name will be given to the congregation and (2) he or she will be removed from fellowship, and (3) he or she will not be given communion.

WORSHIP

First American Methodist Episcopal Church (FAME)
Los Angeles, California

In 1977, Dr. Cecil L. "Chip" Murray became senior pastor of First AME Church (FAME), the oldest black church in Los Angeles. When he assumed the post, he set forth a vision for the church to impact the city. Twenty-seven years later, FAME is a model of community involvement, humanitarian service and dynamic worship.

THE PASTOR

Chip Murray is an articulate visionary who has synthesized the best of black church tradition with a contemporary edge. Murray holds an undergraduate degree from Florida A&M University. He received his Doctorate in Religion from the School of Theology at Clermont, Florida. He has been an adjunct professor at Iliff School of Theology, Seattle University, Claremont School of Theology, Fuller Theological Seminary and Northwest Theological Seminary. Murray has been featured in numerous periodicals including *Time* and *Ebony*. He has also been featured on the *700 Club*, in the *Los Angeles Times* and in other media.

Murray is a compassionate man whose drive for service began early in life. He served for 10 years with the United States Air Force as a jet radar intercept officer and a navigator. He received the Soldier's Medal of Valor in 1958 after an aircraft explosion in his two-seated fighter. This war hero understands that the Church is in a spiritual war with the culture. The military seems to have helped sharpen not only Murray's perceptions but his administrative and leadership gifts as well.

As a result of his unique preparation for ministry and his passion for tangible impact in his community, Murray will definitely leave a lasting legacy. For example, the Hawthorne Shopping Plaza in Los Angeles has erected a sand sculpture as a tribute to African-Americans who are overcomers. The magnificent piece of art features the likeness of George Washington Carver, Harriet Tubman, Phyllis Wheatley, Malcolm X, Martin Luther King, Jr., and Dr. Cecil L. Murray. In addition, President George Herbert Walker Bush named FAME the 177th Point of Light for its courageous outreach in community services. Very few pastors have distinguished themselves so well by both sacred and secular standards.

HISTORY

The African-American Church movement was already more than 100 years old when the FAME story began to unfold. In 1848, as a way to earn freedom, a slave named Biddy Mason herded sheep and cattle from Mississippi to California. As a newly freed woman, she began to work as a nurse, caring for the sick and indigent. She believed that everything she owned belonged to God—that she was simply a steward of what He had given. Therefore, she lived with what she called an "open hand" philosophy. Despite all the other activities she was involved in, Ms. Mason began worship services in her home in Los Angeles. It was through these gatherings that she founded the First African Methodist Episcopal Church in Los Angeles.

FAME was the first black congregation of any kind in the

City of the Angels. FAME's list of distinguished pastors is far too long to enumerate. Suffice it to say that Murray has been instrumental in truly putting the church on the map. Cecil Murray was assigned to the church, as we already have stated, in 1977. It has grown from 300 members to nearly 18,000 members today. The church began with one corporation but now includes 14 distinct corporate entities. These entities employ 180 individuals in 5 general departments. FAME's ministry hosts over 40 programs for the community, including economic development, business training, housing developments, a school and a welfare-to-work program. The annual budget of the entire organization is approximately $12 million.

Notable among the membership are Senator Art Torres, the late Los Angeles Mayor Tom Bradley, Judge Roosevelt Dorn, Judge Irma Brown-Dillon, Arsenio Hall, former Community College Chancellor Dr. Donald Phelps, Dianne Reeves, Michael Warren, Stack Pierce, Mary Wilson and Chauntel Westerman (formerly of *Good Morning America*).

Worship and Church Life

The ministry of FAME is not only marked by its success in social issues, but also the worship services are noted in many articles written about this church. The success of the community outreach is accomplished because of the church's powerful sense of mission and *esprit de corps*. The pastor and key leaders would say that their corporate success emanates from their awe-inspiring spiritual worship service. The impact of their worship inspires and empowers their members to lead 40 task forces that deal with issues including health, substance abuse, homelessness, emergency food and clothing, general and specialized housing, tutoring, entrepreneurial training and employment services. Murray believes that a worship service is not complete unless the congregants have had an experience similar to Isaiah's (see Isa. 6), in which the only logical response can be, "Here am I. Send me!" (v. 8). The benediction of each worship experience should be an invocation for the work that is needed outside the doors of the church.

The hallmark of most African-American worship experiences is typically the music ministry. In our discussions with FAME, they were quick to state that they emphasize the Word of God much more than the musical expressions in the services. Their team sees music as a tool that uplifts people regardless of their circumstances. Music ministry opens the door for the preached Word.

At FAME, excellence and variety mark the music ministry. The choirs and instrumentalists are well rehearsed. There are seven active choirs in the church. Each choir is managed by a different director, which ensures ownership by the choir members and tremendous diversity of style and expression. The youth choir might sing hip-hop music one week and the next week the men's choir might sing a traditional anthem. The pastor is able to choose which group will help him best express the message of the week.

Murray believes that black worship must have a flow from the call to worship to the benediction. He sees it as a drama that flows to a megapoint or "hallelujah point." The call to worship invites the people to come join hands with God and continue through the service with Him. In Murray's mind, there should be one flow from door to door—that is, from entrance to exit.

Each year, Murray establishes a biblical theme for the church. For example, in 2002 the congregation used "Order My Steps." In 2003, the theme was "Thy Will Be Done." Each Sunday becomes one version of the 52 parts of this theme. This keeps everyone focused. The choirs and other groups can prepare based on this theme.

In addition to the annual theme, the weekly song selection is key to congregational participation. FAME music ministers choose songs that are God-ward, centered upon praise and worship, rather than just about the faith. FAME gives the people opportunity to extend their hands and express their love to God. FAME seeks to create moments in which the inner spirit is fed. The worship is in sharp contrast to a purely liturgical approach to music and the Word. Music at FAME leads to altar calls and times of surrender.

The preaching aspect of worship is also a very important element of FAME's Sunday experience. Dr. Murray believes that the preaching must be biblically oriented, relevant and inspiring to the people hearing it. He prepares his sermons using a simple outline—an introduction, a Scripture, a subject, three points and conclusion.

Dr. Murray believes that people must feel the Word of God as deeply as prayer. He believes the Word must be made flesh every time he preaches. This means that people are to do something with what they have heard, the sooner the better. The bulletin helps people know how they can put flesh to the Word. There are over 40 ministry options available to enlist in, so they can spread the Kingdom beyond the walls of the sanctuary. The relevancy of the Word is seen as every member joins a task force. Murray says, "The church is only alive as much as it serves."

FAME's services typically run no longer than 90 minutes. They are carefully planned to fulfill the church's overall goals. Murray expresses these goals in what he calls the 11 commandments of vibrant worship.

1. Worship must flow

   • from the call of worship to the benediction

· to a megapoint—what he calls a hallelujah
point

2. The music must be centered upon praise and
worship.

- Praise and worship are primary.
- God-ward songs must be sung, not just
songs about the faith.
- The Word as music is an emphasis.
- The choirs must be well rehearsed.
- Instrumentalists who accompany the choir
must be well rehearsed.
- Music opens the door for the Word.
- Praise and worship must be uplifting.

3. Limit the number of financial appeals.

- Too many offerings may distract people and
negate the testimony of the church.

4. Announcements and acknowledgments help create
an atmosphere of family.

- Announcements must be used sparingly and
strategically.

5. The Word is the hook of the service.

- The preaching must be biblically oriented.
- The preaching must be relevant and inspiring.

- The preacher must develop a clear theme with an introduction, using Scripture, laying out the subject and presenting it with three points.
- Scripture must relate God to modern life.
- The message must combine grace with judgment.
- Preachers should never leave people under condemnation.
- The lesson must show how to apply grace.
- The altar must be opened for those who seek salvation.
- There must be a challenge presented to the people in the congregation so that they can act upon it.

6. Congregational participation is key.

   - Video projection of announcements and words of songs helps.
   - Churches must seek to make visitors feel that they are welcomed in the service.

7. Keep services thematic.

   - Everyone should be focused.
   - Each Sunday should be 1 step in a 52-step journey.

8. Allow for response.

   - The altar call is a time to surrender.

- People must feel as deeply about the Word as they do about prayer.

9. The Word must be made flesh.

   - Give people ministry options to enlist in beyond the walls of the church.
   - True service begins at the benediction.

10. Don't go on and on.

   - The length of the service is critical to retention.
   - Remember the 90-minute saturation point.

11. Thou **shalt not bore** the people.

   - You must present an exciting Christ.
   - Everyone should have a good time.

Learn more about FAME at www.famechurch.org.

EVANGELISM

SOUL FACTORY
FORESTVILLE, MARYLAND

With a fresh approach to evangelism, the Soul Factory is having the same kind of impact on today's urban African-American youth that Chuck Smith and Calvary Chapel had on the youth of the Jesus movement in the 1970s. Operating from three locations in the greater Washington, D.C., area, the unorthodox church led by Deron Cloud has seen tremendous growth during its eight years.

THE PASTOR

Deron Cloud's father is an attorney and his mother is an ordained minister. This heritage provided a clear analytic approach to his belief system and a tremendous foundation of faith. Nonetheless, Cloud once considered becoming a Black Muslim because of Muslims' commitment to reaching men. Moreover, as a student at the University of Maryland at College Park, Cloud debated the pros and cons of Christianity, yet he eventually realized that a commitment to Christ was the revolutionary move he wanted to make.

Almost immediately after becoming a believer, he started evangelizing others—and he used unique methods, such as drama. At one point he created a one-man play called "The Boyfriend Girlfriend Thang." In his on-stage performance, he hit the hard topics of teen sexuality and abortion—he also got results. Hundreds of teens came to know Christ. As Cloud's impact increased, he discovered that many who had converted under his avant-garde ministry had a difficult time finding a church in which they felt comfortable. They wanted contemporary music and more relevant ministry than what most fellowships offered.

Although Cloud had not initially felt such a call, he soon discerned that God wanted him to pioneer a church where members of the hip-hop subculture could gather. That was the beginning of the Soul Factory. His ministry has since expanded nationally and in 2004 his first book was published by Thomas Nelson.

History

After Cloud knew he was to start a church but before he actually planted the Soul Factory—originally called the Church of the Lord's Disciples—he read as many books on church growth as he could get his hands on. Through his research he concluded that the church in America was rapidly becoming culturally irrelevant. He was particularly influenced by Rick Warren's *The Purpose-Driven Church,* which he still turns to regularly.

The Soul Factory was founded as a home Bible study in 1995 and held its first regular church service in a rented auditorium in September 1996. After 2 months in the auditorium, the congregation moved into a 2,000-square-foot storefront in Forestville, Maryland. By the second week the new facility was so packed that an interior wall had to be knocked down to make more room. Within 2 years, the congregation passed the 500 mark in regular attendance.

Cloud uses drama as his primary evangelism strategy outside the church. His presentations aim to match the quality of stand-up comedy acts on Black Entertainment Television or in comedy clubs. Pastor Cloud has recently begun to take his plays on the road. A team of nearly 50 church volunteers has been mobilized to travel to Baltimore, Dallas, Houston and Virginia Beach. In each city, thousands of people jam into rented auditoriums and each night hundreds accept Christ for the first time.

Toward the end of the church's second year, Cloud started to implement some of the principles put forth in George Barna's book *Team Leadership*. He assembled a team of people who he felt could lead the church. After rebuilding the pioneer leadership team, Cloud's next step was to lease enough space in a mall to accommodate his vision. The mall was well suited for the dramatic outreach. One thousand people showed up for the first service in the new venue. Within 5 years, 2,300 people were attending Soul Factory each Sunday. In desperate need of more space, the church opened a second campus about 15 miles away in Washington, D.C., and a third campus about 22 miles to the southeast, in Waldorf, Maryland. Today nearly 5,000 people worship each Sunday at the three Soul Factory campuses.

After six years, the leadership decided to change the name of the church. They wanted to avoid turning off new converts with a religious-sounding name. Soul Factory was chosen because it describes the church's step-by-step process of ministry. The word "factory" implies both predictability and purpose. The nonpretentious sound of the new name exudes the church's mission for hands-on impact. The Soul Factory's self-described mission is to bring the message of God's love and deliverance to people who are devoid of Christ and bring them into relationship with God and His family. To that end, Cloud and his team seek to bring God's timeless truths to the masses through innovative and relevant strategies. They want to make God *real* to each person they encounter.

BEST PRACTICES

The Soul Factory has developed a unique corporate culture. It looks more like a mission with zeal than a traditional, slow-paced church. The Soul Factory targets lower- and middle-class African-Americans between the ages of 18 and 35 and seeks to help them build positive, Christlike relationships with each other.

There are seven principles upon which the church operates.

1. A Clear Evangelistic Philosophy

It may be surprising to some to learn that Sunday-morning services are not the key ingredient to winning souls at the Soul Factory. Though there is quite a lot of prayer at the altar, most of the evangelism is left to the cell groups. The philosophy is to bring Jesus to where the people are.

The Soul Factory's philosophy of evangelism is summed up by the phrase "keep it real." Cloud recommends that pastors glory in their personal weaknesses. He believes that he needs to let the people know that he goes through the same thing they go through, just in different areas of his life. Transparency doesn't present a perfect picture of the walk with Christ. In life, he says, there are ups and down, but everyone can overcome such setbacks—it just takes effort and responsibility.

Cloud candidly speaks about specific obstacles to overcome within the black community. He believes that there is a great deal of anger within people in the black culture. Issues of abandonment and neglect are prevalent, he notes. These issues are usually best understood by other African-Americans. This is why evangelistic efforts by people from other racial groups who attempt to go inside the black community usually fail.

2. Financial Commitment to Evangelism

The Soul Factory designates 60 percent of its church budget toward evangelistic efforts. Cloud attributes the numeric growth of the church to the effective plays that the church presents. Drama is different from preaching. It can be used to shock, evoke tears, produce camaraderie and help people in the audience identify with sin. The effectiveness of drama brings people to a point of sincere confession and repentance. The congregation sees the evidence of the fruit and then invites others to share in the experience.

3. Constant Improvement of Outreach

Pastor Cloud has trained others to assist him in dramatic evangelism. This is a group that he personally supervises. Group members are encouraged to participate in the planning for each season's evangelistic outreaches. The dramatic outreaches utilize state-of-the-art video technology, professional costumes, innovative props and advanced theater lighting. After each drama, the pastor makes an altar call for salvation and for those who are in need of prayer. Usually 80 percent of the audience stands in response. Sometimes more than 1,000 people rise.

4. A Clear Discipleship Strategy

Pastor Cloud believes that the biweekly cell-group meetings are fundamental to church growth. The Soul Factory has a 75 percent small-group participation rate, which is high when compared to most churches that use similar strategies. At first, the Soul Factory modeled its small groups after David Yonghi Cho's design—Cho is pastor of one of the world's largest churches, Yoido Full Gospel Church in Seoul, South Korea. Soul Factory has also augmented the group experience with program material and principles gleaned from other small groups, thus creating its own style.

The church points people to the cell groups as a fundamental resource for relationships. Pastor Cloud addresses the relationships within the family by preaching from the pulpit on issues of dysfunction. He usually offers self-help tips, too. Small-group members then discuss the sermon from the previous Sunday.

Members find it easier to share the gospel with others in the comfort of a home. Each small group hosts two evangelistic outreaches per year. Another benefit of the cell groups is that they become like a therapy group in which people have the freedom to talk about their problems without the fear of being ostracized. Pastor Cloud believes this makes his job much easier, because people help each other and do not look so much in his direction.

5. Concert Outreach

The Soul Factory uses two types of concerts as vehicles for outreach: jazz for adults and GoGo for youth.

Jazz

Called All that Jazz, the concerts occur once a month. They take place in a clublike setting—but without smoke or alcohol. The people mingle, enjoy the music and eat a lot of food.

Nearly 700 people attended the first All that Jazz night. Many wives gave testimony that their unsaved husbands came. Non-Christian music groups are invited to play, but they are not allowed to address the crowd between songs. These groups usually play some gospel jazz and other hits. Some of these artists have received salvation during their time at All that Jazz.

GoGo

GoGo music nights attract youth. GoGo music is a unique urban style of music birthed on the East Coast and is widely played and listened to in the Washington, D.C., area. The church began this outreach by hiring a top-notch GoGo band and advertising the event internally. The crowd was by invitation only. Each youth was given two invitations—one for him- or herself and one for an unsaved friend.

6. Targeted Youth Discipleship

As the Soul Factory has grown, its leaders have recognized the need for a specialized youth ministry. They call it Young SOLDIERS. "SOLDIER" is an acronym for "Sold Out, Living, Delivered, In Everlasting Righteous Service." The Young SOLDIERS meet every Thursday. In addition to weekly gatherings, youth frequently go on retreats to the ministry's 50-acre youth facility. In the summer, the youth facility is used for longer camps and urban kids are invited to a boot camp-like venue where they can learn personal discipline and biblical principles.

7. Small-Group Outreach Events

The Soul Factory invests a lot of creativity and planning in small-group outreach events. One unique approach to serving multiple cell groups is to host a churchwide Heavy Hitter Event. The event consists of group games and activities with an object lesson. Each team of people might have a fun project to do together. For example, each team might be asked to build a contraption that can toss an egg as far as possible. At the end of the evening, a call to discipleship is given. The church typically invites 200 to 300 people to each event.

CLOUD'S ADVICE

Pastor Deron Cloud offers to pastors who want to implement these seven principles four specific pieces of advice:

1. Spend your money on the people, not real estate.
2. Think outside the box. Try to be relevant. Don't evaluate your success by typical church standards.
3. Go with your gut. Don't try to duplicate the church experience—that will come in time.
4. Have a very close support network, people who will tell you the truth and people with whom you can dream.

You can find out more about the Soul Factory at www.deroncloud.org.

FAMILY

CHRISTIAN STRONGHOLD BAPTIST CHURCH
PHILADELPHIA, PENNSYLVANIA

Dr. Willie Richardson founded Christian Stronghold Baptist Church in 1966. The name was chosen because "stronghold" is a military term meaning "fort" or "fortress." A stronghold is a place where soldiers are both trained and find safety. In Richardson's thinking, the stronghold also becomes a place of healing for those who have been wounded in battle. After receiving care and regaining their strength, soldiers can be sent back into battle.

Richardson has been faithful to his Philadelphia post for more than 38 years. During this time the church has attempted to respond to the ever-changing needs of the people in the church and in the surrounding community—which not only includes urban Philadelphia but also now extends to a four-state region.

Stronghold began a Bible institute in 1974, which conducts classes on Sunday evenings and seeks to equip believers as they mature in their faith. During the last decade or so, the training has been adapted to include areas of practical living, too.

THE PASTOR

Dr. Willie Richardson was a mechanical design engineer in research and development before he became a pastor. As he familiarized himself with local-church ministries, he determined to use his professional disciplines in the context of ministry. His greatest passion in church development has always been ministry to the family. In 1977, he and his wife, Patricia, created Christian Research and Development (CRD), which specializes in addressing issues that affect black families. This institute develops materials for churches, including biblical counseling guidelines, family-ministry tools and evangelism instruction.

The Richardsons have passed along their knowledge to hundreds of pastors, helping them to reach out to thousands of African-American families nationwide. The couple has received national recognition for their work, culminating in White House invitations from President Ronald Reagan, President George Herbert Walker Bush and President George W. Bush.

Richardson believes that the church can target black males in the community and win them to Christ; this was the subject of his book *How to Get Men in the Church and Keep Most of Them*. In this work, he discusses three basic strategies: rapport, evangelism and discipleship. Powerful principles for developing families are shared in three additional books: *The Black Family, Past, Present and Future*; *Discipling the City*; and *Reclaiming the Urban Family*.

His gift of teaching has put Richardson in great demand with educators. He has served as a professor of urban theological studies for Westminster Theological Seminary, Philadelphia College of the Bible and Messiah College. He is chairman of the board of trustees for the Center for Urban Theological Studies in Philadelphia and serves on several other prestigious boards.

EQUIPPING THE CHILDREN

Christian Stronghold has a firm commitment to families. This focus led to the start of the Creative World Learning Center in 1993, which provides day care for toddlers and infants in a safe and loving Christlike environment where children can develop spiritually, emotionally and physically.

From the start, the Creative World Learning Center took in toddlers and infants from the community, not just from the families of church members. The day care was so effective that parents asked the church leadership to begin an elementary school. The Christian Stronghold Learning Academy was founded in 1997. In addition, the church has "adopted" a secular school, enabling it to help children in the community who cannot attend the church's school.

A Growing Church

In nearly four decades of ministry, Christian Stronghold has grown to 4,000 members. Richardson attributes most of this expansion to personal evangelism. Seventy percent of the congregation had never before attended any other church or were "lapsed Christians" prior to coming to Stronghold. This is an unusually high percentage of people who had fallen out of regular church attendance—people whom George Barna calls "unchurched."[1]

Given the great degree of brokenness in the urban black family, Christian Stronghold needed to create innovative ways of recruiting and discipling its membership. Church Family Cells were designed to strengthen families by modeling values and facilitating personal accountability.

Family Ministry

For the first 10 years of his ministry, Richardson promoted the idea that once a Christian couple said their vows, the power of the Scriptures would automatically help them create a good marriage. However, as he watched many singles select the wrong mate—even when both were Christians—he began to rethink his approach. Premarital training became a prelude to a strong family ministry. In *Reclaiming the Urban Family*, Richardson laid out the strategy.[2] He recommends five fundamental dimensions a church needs to incorporate if it is to have an effective family ministry:

1. Start when people are single.
2. Disciple strategically both men and women.
3. Equip people for marriage.
4. Include crisis intervention and counseling.
5. Minister to children and youth.

Christian Stronghold's leaders teach that the family is the foundation of our walk with God. Jesus is our Brother, God is our Father, and other believers are our brothers and sisters. From the leaders' perspective, we cannot understand Christianity without a clear concept of the family. Dr. Richardson annually preaches a 12-week series on family life. He also includes a 4-week series on single life.

Teaching alone is not enough. Healthy relationships must also be modeled. Therefore, entire families—from the youngest to the oldest—are welcome in the cell groups. Adults take turns supervising the children, who usually gather in a separate room. Singles are also encouraged to come. In fact, many college-aged singles are invited to spend the holidays with families in their cell groups.

1. Start when people are single

Christian Stronghold teaches singles how to develop strong relationships. Becoming someone's friend is much more difficult than falling into the stereotypical role of boyfriend/girlfriend or lover. The church's teachings deal with the question: How do you relate to members of the opposite sex in appropriate ways?

Singles must unlearn many behaviors accepted by the culture at large. The church recognizes that there is a crisis among single Christian women because they feel they must get married by a certain point in life. This mind-set can lead to many emotional pressures and in some cases relational competition and immorality. Many single women have not had nurturing relationships with fathers and brothers. Therefore, they have not experienced *safe* male love.

Christian Stronghold provides opportunities for singles to learn how to be friends. During singles retreats they hear guest speakers. In addition, they are given practical training on how to develop godly relationships. The church hosts events that allows singles to meet and interact with each other in a supportive environment. Christian Stronghold does not endorse the traditional concept of one-on-one dating. Group activities and double dates are recommended in order to avoid the temptations of premarital sex. Often singles meet at church. This allows a person's Christian friends to evaluate a potential suitor.

2. Disciple strategically both men and women

As soon as a person decides to follow Christ, he or she is assigned a brother or sister for 12 weeks. First the new convert is established in the fundamentals of the faith. Next he or she is encouraged to join a gender-specific discipleship group. Men's discipleship and women's discipleship groups are designed to help each person, whether married or single, to mature in his or her concept of relationship. These groups encourage single people to make a spiritual relationship with their friends first and as priority. Only after the relationship has developed should a believer consider whether it is leading to marriage. On the other hand, married people are given basic relationship training to ensure the smooth functioning of their existing commitment. This approach is a vital measure to prevent future familial problems.

In this context, men are taught to be brave, to take initiative and to be the primary problem solvers. They learn to do this within the context of the family, the neighborhood and the community. As a cell church, the neighborhoods are being reached and then men need to be proactive. Women also receive specialized discipleship, equipping them for their unique role in the family and society.

3. Equip people for marriage

Christian Stronghold equips its members by offering premarital counseling and special classes.

People who desire to be married are required to complete 16 weeks of premarital counseling. The church's counselors are so experienced that they usually can predict major issues that will occur within the marriage. One year after the wedding, each couple must complete a follow-up counseling period.

In addition, Stronghold's Bible Institute offers practical living classes on many topics, including communication, finances, sexual issues and conflict management. The combination of classes, family cell groups and gender-specific discipleship groups provides optimum training and support for married couples. In addition to these ongoing opportunities, the church offers seminars and retreats.

4. Include crisis intervention and counseling

Christian Stronghold started the National Association of Biblical Counselors. This began in response to a growing number of queries from various churches that sought working models of successful ministry to African-American families.

Christian Stronghold attempts to give to others everything it has learned over decades of ministry.

At one point, Pastor Richardson and an associate put a revolutionary concept of hands-on intervention to a test. They started with three of the worst families in the church and tracked the effectiveness of ministry for a decade. Each family included men who were drug addicts and women who were illiterate. Most included teenaged children. Richardson and his team personally met with the members of each family and coached them as they made career decisions. On a practical level, they sent the men and women to the church's career enrichment program. At a deeper level, they confronted attitudes about success and racism.

This process and its success led Christian Stronghold to create a full-time ministry called Circle of Light, which works with the neediest of families. Started in 1995, it acts like a SWAT team to embrace and care for the family.

5. Minister to children and youth

Christian Stronghold designates a lot of financial and physical resources to meeting the needs of children and youth. The church's philosophy is to support the family, not replace it. Following this maxim, the church does not have a formal rite-of-passage program because it deems such programs more Afrocentric than Christian. A grassroots program that invites church members to serve as spiritual "uncles" and "aunts" better serves youth as they move through their adolescent years. These uncles and aunts are invited each year to the family home for the youth's birthday party. During this event, they speak to the child about the next steps in his or her life. These are mentors whom the child can talk to as he or she grows up. The uncles and aunts often become a part of the youth's friendship circle.

STEWARDSHIP

NEW BIRTH MISSIONARY BAPTIST CHURCH
LITHONIA, GEORGIA

In 1984, 150 people led by Rev. Kenneth Samuel decided to begin a church in Decatur, Georgia. They chose New Birth Missionary Baptist Church as a name. In 1987, the congregation asked Eddie L. Long to become its pastor. Under Long's leadership, New Birth grew spiritually, economically and numerically. In January 1991, the church dedicated its facility, which was valued at more than $2 million.

THE PASTOR

Bishop Eddie L. Long is the senior pastor of New Birth Missionary Baptist. The son of a preacher, he resisted the temptation to simply follow tradition. Today, his ministry has become synonymous with innovation, effectiveness and authenticity.

Bishop Long earned a B.A. in business administration from North Carolina Central University and a M.Div. degree from Atlanta's Interdenominational Theological Center. He is the author of *Power of a Wise Woman; What a Man Wants, What a Woman Needs; Called to Conquer; Taking Over;* and *I Don't Want Delilah, I Need You.* He has received many honors.

- He is listed among America's 125 most influential leaders.
- He received the 1999 Legacy Award from Big Brothers

Big Sisters of Metro Atlanta.

- He received the 2003 Leadership: Faith/Community Award from 100 Black Men of America.
- *Savoy* magazine selected him as one of the most influential blacks in America in 2003.
- He received the 2003 Champion Award for Spiritual Enlightenment from All Children Are Special, Inc.

In addition to these awards, Bishop Long serves on several boards, including the board of trustees for Young Life, board of visitors for Emory University, board of trustees for North Carolina Central University and as vice-chairman of the Morehouse School of Religion board of directors.

In 1994, Bishop Long was consecrated as the third presiding bishop of the Full Gospel Baptist Church Fellowship. He took a bold stance when he publicly challenged the Nation of Islam-led Million Man March in October of 1995. Today he leads his own network of ministers and participates in both the National Baptist Convention and the American Baptist Convention.

HISTORY

By 1992, New Birth had grown to more than 8,000 members. Over the next two years, the church established many ministries, including a Christian school called Faith Academy and Project Destiny, a comprehensive family-restoration program that provides services to youth and their families. Project Destiny offers family crisis intervention, life-skills classes, help for troubled kids who need to reenter school and other programs.

In 1995, New Birth began its weekly television broadcast *Taking Authority*. This program is currently seen in more than

170 countries. In the Atlanta area, the church airs both television and radio broadcasts.

In 1997, New Birth joined with several area churches to open the South DeKalb Federal Church Credit Union—to enable members to receive personal and business loans.

New Birth's current facilities are situated on a 240-acre parcel of land. A $50 million complex features a 10,000-seat sanctuary, administrative offices, a library, a bookstore, a computer lab, a kitchen, audio and video studios, a nursery and more. Today, the church has more than 25,000 members, making it one of the largest churches in the nation.

BEST PRACTICES

New Birth's strength of stewardship is fundamentally based upon its teachings about the kingdom of God and mature Christian living. Seeing Christ's invisible kingdom manifested on Earth has become a passion for Bishop Long.

New Birth's teaching about the kingdom of God springs out of the leadership team's belief that Adam was originally created to rule, subdue and have dominion. The second Adam, Jesus, came to restore humankind to a place of spiritual dominion, in which believers rule and reign with Christ. There is a spiritual militancy to this worldview. This take-charge presentation of Christianity is tempered by the values of love and servanthood.

New Birth emphasizes five realms in which the kingdom of God should have progressive dominion: in individual hearts and lives, in family relationships, in the marketplace, in the government and in the world. Bishop Long teaches that Christians have been placed in the world today in order to bring the influence of the Kingdom into their unique spheres of influence. Years before Rick Warren's book *The Purpose-Driven Life* made the best-seller's list, Bishop Long was teaching very similar concepts. In his mind, Christianity is not about church services; rather, it is about expanding the rule and reign of Christ in the world. This gives new dignity to people at every level of society. Even the factory worker comes to understand that his or her work can influence others by presenting the character of Christ in the workplace and helping others to make decisions based on biblical principles.

As New Birth members begin to understand their unique role in God's kingdom, they instinctively desire to invest their time, talent and treasure into the kingdom of God. The financial result for the church is an annual income of approximately $30 million. This high level of giving reflects personal ownership of the church's dynamic vision. New Birth's stewardship philosophy will not work in every setting, yet there are four principles listed below that any church can adopt.

1. Cast a Compelling Vision

The leadership team at New Birth believes that the vision must constantly be set before the congregation. The members of its leadership team work with an understanding that they are trying to create a unique corporate culture and membership mindset. Therefore, Bishop Long does not preach many messages on stewardship as an isolated topic; rather, he mentions it often in the normal flow of church life.

Bishop Long's philosophy on stewardship has evolved over the years. At first he did not buy himself new cars nor did he take up an offering at every service. Why? He did not want to be seen as a leader who was always taking people's money or spending extravagantly. Over time, he has realized that giving is an avenue of blessing for his people. The Bible encourages lifestyle stewardship, which includes financial giving. Therefore, Bishop Long has come to understand that a leader must help his church members excel in the "grace of giving" (2 Cor. 8:7). Today Bishop Long and his team make no apologies for encouraging everyone to invest his or her own time, talent and treasure into New Birth's vision.

2. Develop a Team to Lead Fund-Raising Efforts

A team works with the senior pastor to raise awareness about the church's financial projects. The New Birth chief financial officer is extremely gifted and has developed a council that helps him organize fund-raising strategies in conjunction with Bishop Long. In addition, highly professional videos and printed materials are often produced to support the church's financial campaigns.

The majority of New Birth's finances come from tithes and offerings, yet money is raised in other ways as well. For example, corporate sponsorships and grants are sought outside of the church. Within the church, there is a wide array of things that bring in money. Most ministries raise a certain amount of money to offset their ministry expenses. The youth have fund-raisers, the Life Bible Institute has registration fees and book fees, and audiocassette revenues are used to fund a scholarship program at the church.

3. Model Excellence in Corporate Stewardship

Many churches could be accused of telling people to do what they say instead of doing what they do. This is not the case with New Birth, in the financial/stewardship arena. The church uses superior stewardship approaches in order to reach its financial goals. This modeling is done in the following ways:

- **They have excellent financial systems in place.** There is an internal audit twice a year from an independent company. Full disclosure is made of the church budget and its line items of expenses.

- **The church has been very successful in managing the church's real-estate investments.** In 1996, the church was able to purchase 170 acres of prime property worth over $10 million for only $3 million. Later that year, after selling the 170 acres acquired, the church made a profit of $11 million. With this profit, they were able to purchase over 240 acres for a new multimillion dollar church complex, pay all church debts and deposit $2 million in the bank.
- **The church is developing entrepreneurs to impact the community.** The New Birth Entrepreneur school is part of the Kingdom message, occupy until He returns (see Luke 19:13). Christian businesspeople are taught that they should be taking spoils from the kingdom of darkness and building up Christ's kingdom. The Entrepreneur school is teaching emerging leaders how to start and maintain godly businesses. Classes deal with nitty-gritty issues, such as setting standards in the workplace. What does the church expect to gain from this training? The church wants the people who graduate from the school to be catalysts who help other members get started in business the right way.

4. Develop Creative Volunteer Recruitment Strategies

Recognizing that financial management is not the only aspect of stewardship, New Birth has sought to present a compelling vision of personal development through service to its members. New Birth hosts Super Saturdays for new members, which are designed to orient the people to the church. The call for involvement is first issued here. Besides this, they have Modules for

New Members, which teach the church's philosophy and vision and ways new members can connect. Profiles are administered in order to determine each person's placement. Spiritual job fairs are conducted by representatives from the ministries. This entire process is overseen by the volunteer services department.

New Birth has done an excellent job of addressing the six primary factors that motivate people to make an investment in a local church. These factors are (1) shared cause, (2) ministry effectiveness, (3) ministry influence, (4) urgent need, (5) personal benefit and (6) relationship with the ministry.

Find out more about New Birth Missionary Baptist Church at www.newbirth.org.

COMMUNITY

WEST ANGELES CHURCH OF GOD IN CHRIST
LOS ANGELES, CALIFORNIA

West Angeles Church of God in Christ began as a storefront church in 1943 in the heart of Los Angeles. For 25 years it remained a small congregation, only booming in attendance after the arrival of Bishop Charles E. Blake in 1968. Today it is recognized as one of the largest and fastest-growing churches in the nation, with extensive community and media outreach.

THE PASTOR

When Bishop Blake was appointed pastor, the average Sunday attendance was about 50. Today West Angeles claims 22,000 members, occupies a 5,000-seat sanctuary and extends its ministry into the community and around the world. Over three decades, Bishop Blake has become one of the true statesmen of the African-American church. He has a gentle, caring spirit, yet he also wields great authority in the community and in his denomination.

Bishop Blake grew up in Southern California and stepped into ministry under the tutelage of his father, the late Bishop J. A. Blake. He received a B.A. from California Western University and a M.Div. from Interdenominational Theological Center. Through the years, many groups have honored Bishop Blake, including the Salvation Army (the William Booth award), the Greenlining Institute (the Big Heart award) and the Los Angeles Urban League (the Whitney M. Young award). He has written many books, including *Free to Dream*.

Bishop Blake currently serves as first assistant presiding bishop and on the presiding board of the Church of God in Christ denomination, which is based in Memphis, Tennessee. He is also the jurisdictional prelate in Southern California, overseeing more than 220 churches.

THE CONGREGATION

During the 1970s, along with rapid growth in attendance, West Angeles expanded in other ways, some of which took the church into territory unfamiliar to most African-American congregations at the time. For example, in 1976, the church founded West Angeles Christian Academy. Today the school serves 226 students from kindergarten through grade 8 and is accredited.

In 1981, the West Angeles congregation moved to 3405 Crenshaw Boulevard (now known as its north campus). From this ministry hub Bishop Blake and his team have reached out to people in diverse groups, from the "least of these" in society to celebrities such as Denzel Washington, Stevie Wonder, Angela Bassett and Magic Johnson (all regular attendees).

More than 175 employees and more than 1,000 volunteers serve through about 80 specialized ministries, programs and support groups. West Angeles impacts the community in many ways, including stimulating the local economy by generating more than $16 million in annual income.

BEST PRACTICES

Many African-American churches operate a Community Development Corporation (CDC), which can receive grants and funds from foundations and businesses. These funds go toward creating viable faith-based social services. A CDC is a link between the church and the greater community.

West Angeles's Community Development Corporation was founded in early 1994 and is directed by Dr. Lula Balton. Today it is recognized as one of the most productive in California, specifically in offering food services and emergency relief. Its skid-row ministry serves more than 5,000 meals each month to homeless and disadvantaged persons. Food is also given to needy families. The CDC's community dispute-resolution and legal services, in partnership with Pepperdine University Law School, provides legal services for moderate-income people who would not otherwise qualify for legal aid.

West Angeles also helps low- and middle-income residents achieve self-sufficiency through home ownership. Through Individual Development Accounts (IDA) people are able to move out of poverty by augmenting existing assets. A person's possessions of value (house, car or money in the bank) are supplemented based on a 3-to-1 basis and placed in an IDA savings account. The IDA funds can be used to purchase a home, start or expand a business or pay for tuition for postsecondary education.

Balton and the West Angeles CDC teams see their work as a process to liberate individuals spiritually and then to bring them economic empowerment, social justice and community transformation. All of this is done under Jesus' mandate to go into the entire world and make disciples (see Matt. 28:19).

With a strategy that equips people for lasting employment, the West Angeles CDC assists people in their search for work, helps them acquire financial aid for career development and trains them in corporate etiquette. It also partners with community leaders, business leaders and residents on specific projects, which create career opportunities. Moreover, the CDC actively pursues partnerships with banks and financial institutions to gain the funding needed to rehabilitate old homes, build afford-able housing or obtain preferred mortgage rates for first-time home owners.

Social justice is another major thrust. The CDC seeks to raise the awareness of how people can shape their own future. Specific tactics include the promotion of educational initiatives, including literacy among adults. The CDC promotes English as a second language, which meets a need in the growing Hispanic population in the West Angeles neighborhood.

Justice does not end with community institutions. Often individuals need a method of personal mediation that does not involve the expense of the traditional legal system. The West Angeles CDC participates in local activities that have the ability to foster structural justice. West Angeles believes that social jus-tice is a responsibility of the church as an agent of the kingdom of God. Therefore, it facilitates this kind of justice through a program called Community Dispute Resolution. This program helps opposing groups and individuals understand reconcilia-tion in real-life situations and reach positive resolutions.

West Angeles Church of God in Christ is doing so many good things that it is hard to highlight just a few practices that other churches should follow. Here are 10 examples:

- **Administration/community services.** This is an advocacy for social, legislative and economic issues. Quarterly, West Angeles holds Law Days, offering free legal services. The church also provides free income-tax assistance. Other activities include education to pre-vent domestic violence.
- **Mediation center.** Serving as the peacemaker arm of the CDC, this aspect of ministry provides crosscultural

mediation in disputes between neighbors, families, landlords and tenants, schools and students, employees and employers, merchants and consumers, and business partners.

- **Affordable housing developments.** The CDC operates homes for large families and apartments for families with children and is currently pursuing development for seniors.
- **Home-ownership initiatives.** The CDC provides home-buyer education and training. It acquires single-family residences to rehab and sell to families of low- to moderate-income levels. It also includes a prequalifying mortgage service for prospective home buyers.
- **Community assistance.** This division provides emergency services for people and families. It offers a senior-care program, a food co-op, a food-share program, energy assistance and referrals for housing and jobs.
- **Economic development.** This part of the CDC offers assistance to small businesses and entrepreneurs in creation of business, technical areas, business stimulation and expansion. It also has commercial development projects.
- **Welfare-to-Work.** This is a faith-based program called Empower. This overall case management service encompasses outreach to welfare recipients, intake and assessment of needs, the development of basic life skills, training in job-related skills, job placement and follow-up for job retention.
- **Support-group meetings.** Linking ministries of the church to the community, this aspect of the CDC taps the West Angeles substance abuse committee Free 'N' One ministry; the codependent Tough Love ministry;

the marriage-recovery support group for those who are divorced or separated; the Law Enforcement/Fire Service Fellowship; the grief and bereavement support group Bridging the Gap; the deaf and hard of hearing ministry; the singles ministry; the caregivers support group; the marriage-maintenance ministry; the Effective Fathering Fellowship; the Solo Parenting ministry; and Couples for Christ.

- **Classes.** This is another link between West Angeles and the CDC. Classes are offered in the areas of anger management, premarital counseling, single parenting, distance learning, biblical counseling within the urban context and more.

- **Counseling center services.** This center has a multitude of clinics on finance, preparation for marriage, parenting, child therapy, personality-profile testing, stress reduction and more. It provides counseling services for codependency, divorce and separation, marriage enhancement, HIV/AIDS support and other needs.

For more information, visit West Angeles's website at www.westa.org.

RELATIONSHIPS

LONG REACH CHURCH OF GOD
COLUMBIA, MARYLAND

The Church of God discussed planting a church in the new city of Columbia, Maryland, in 1972. A few families began meeting monthly for Bible study in the home of Robert and Doris Davis. The first worship service was held in January of 1973. Dr. Robert S. Davis, Sr., served as chairman of the congregation at its inception, supporting John Stanley, the first pastor of the church. The church began with 30 committed people.

In the fall of 1975, the congregation called Robert Davis to serve as senior pastor. Home Bible studies were instituted that would later be called Growth Groups. Within a year, church membership grew by 75 percent. Throughout the next few years, the church sought to find a permanent place of corporate worship. During this season, the Growth Groups were pivotal in keeping Long Reach's membership together. Therefore, these groups also became instrumental in pastoral care and laid the groundwork for the continued growth in church attendance.

THE PASTOR

Robert S. Davis, Sr., is senior pastor of Long Reach Church of God. He is a caring man who loves people and has desired to create a church with a depth of both fellowship and discipleship.

Pastor Davis holds a B.S. from West Virginia State College, a M.Div. from Howard University and a Ph.D. in ministry from Regent University School of Divinity. He worked as a forensic chemist in the Baltimore City Police Department prior to entering full-time ministry.

His regional leadership includes serving as an executive board member of both Project Bridges (a regional multichurch economic and church developmental organization) in metropolitan Washington, D.C., and One Church/One Child, serving the Baltimore metropolitan area. He was consecrated a bishop by the Church of God in Anderson, Indiana, and has served on its leadership council and the four-member cabinet. Bishop Davis also ministers widely as a cell-church specialist and serves as a member of the Touch Outreach board of directors in Houston, Texas.

History

In 1985, the church dedicated a new church building, after four years of intense planning and fund-raising. Long Reach became the first church in Columbia, Maryland, to build its own place of worship. This was quite a feat. Columbia, Maryland, began in 1967 as an award-winning 14,000-acre planned community. The city's creators had provided corporate spaces for worship designed to accommodate multiple congregations sharing the same building. However, the municipality did not make planning or zoning provisions for more traditional individual church building locations. In many ways, Long Reach was a pioneer in a new kind of church plant. The challenges of developing a dynamic ministry in Columbia in those days were similar to those faced by emerging churches all over the nation today. Church facilities and manpower to build were either very expensive or inaccessible. Creativity was needed to bring the church to a critical mass that could afford to break into the real-estate market and secure permanent facilities.

Long Reach quickly abandoned the concept of Growth Groups, shifting to a Home Bible Class. This change allowed the church to bring needed foundational Bible teaching to a growing community of Christians who were eager to learn and grow. The church had grown to about 200 members when it entered a new facility.

In 1991, the church had to make adjustments to embrace the metachurch model of ministry espoused by Carl George and others. This gave birth to 20 Home Fellowship Groups. In 1996, the church held its first cell conference. In 1997, Davis further introduced the innovative G-12 model of small groups, popularized in South America. During the same period, Long Reach created a Bible training center, which helped people in personal development and cell leadership.

Today, Long Reach Church of God continues to base its ministry on relational values. The cell groups have changed in structure over the years, but they have never strayed from their purpose: to build community among individuals inside the church family and to evangelize the neighborhood. There are now 80 cell groups and a total membership of 1,200 people.

BEST PRACTICES

Long Reach has learned many radical lessons about developing relationships in a changing city. Suzanne Haley, a staff member who has been with the church many years, has helped us understand the four keys to the success of Long Reach Church of God's small-group ministry.

Flexible Structure

When the leadership team members of Long Reach think about their history, they remember significant transitions that helped them seize major opportunities. The Growth Groups of the early church days brought stabilization. The Bible-centered, felt-need focus attracted many people. As the church grew, the leadership recognized they needed to preserve emotional and relational intimacy within the church. The leaders realized a major management principle espoused by Harvard Business School's renowned professor of leadership John P. Cotter. He stated that an organization that successfully leads people through change does eight things very well. Long Reach and other well-managed groups typically follow their own version of these steps.

1. Create a sense of urgency.
2. Put together a strong team to direct the process.
3. Create an appropriate vision.
4. Communicate the new vision broadly.
5. Empower employees to act on the vision.
6. Produce short-term results to give their efforts and to disempower the cynics.
7. Build momentum and use that momentum to tackle tougher change problems.
8. Anchor the new behavior in organizational culture.[1]

Leadership Development

The small-group system of Long Reach Church was very structured and the leaders received training to care for the people. The leaders were empowered to provide pastoral care, a component that had been missing from the growing church's climate. At one point, Long Reach had about 200 cells operating within the church. Unfortunately, the church could not develop leadership quickly enough in order to expand the number of cell groups. Columbia, Maryland, at this time was an extremely transient community. Although now many people live and die within the city, it was only founded, as we mentioned earlier, in 1969. Therefore, leadership development at Long Reach has been the pivotal hinge upon which church growth has swung back and forth.

In the early days, Long Reach's training may have been perceived as legalistic, almost militaristic. This rigidity began to affect the sense of family and teamwork they had endeavored so hard to build. Therefore, the church created a 26-week program that emphasized training, based on mentoring relationships. During the next 5 years, the church leadership team became very stable. They sought to grow the ministry at a manageable rate.

The small-group ministry had become a managerial boot camp for most of the leaders at Long Reach Church of God. The community value that they held so dear in the early days had now been transferred to almost every department of the church because of the investment in the small-group leadership.

A Strategic Mission Audit

As Columbia grew, the church attracted people from all walks of life. These people also had myriad needs and expectations. Columbia, Maryland, of the '90s was a far cry from the Columbia, Maryland, of the '70s. The leadership team awoke to the fact that their community had dramatically changed right before their eyes. Unlike thousands of urban churches whose ethnicity changed as they just watched their numbers dwindle down to nothing, Long Reach decided to review the new community demographics, to develop a new overall strategy for reaching them and to set a new course for the church's future.

Their strategy audit led them to Rick Warren's *The Purpose-Driven Church*. This book helped them understand how to reengineer their church. From Warren's writings they began to understand that every church had people in one of five levels:

Community, Crowd, Congregation, Committed and Core. The Long Reach leadership determined that a cell group was better for the serious people—those at the Congregation or Committed level. Unfortunately, they felt that hundreds of people to whom they had been ministering would not get to the Committed level unless drastic changes were made in the church. Since many Columbians were affluent, upwardly mobile people who were satisfied with a "Sunday Morning Christianity," the team decided it would make a commitment to reach its Jerusalem for Christ.

Therefore, they set forth the following plan: They continued to disciple a church within the church. They would be open to evangelizing the church-exposed community with a clear plan to lead them into deeper levels of Christian commitment. In their thinking, it appeared to be difficult for a "program-based" church to transition into a cell-group based (relationship-oriented) ministry. But they concluded that it would be easy for a cell-based church to spread community through its ministries. Today, the ministries at Long Reach Church are saturated with a majority of their people who are in cell groups—but they are reaching out with a unique structure to impact their entire city.

Targeted Small Groups

Our research team asked the church's leaders about the differences in how relationships are made and developed between urban and suburban churches. This is the crux of the problem that Long Reach Church of God's leadership team has had to address. In their opinion, most black churches in the North have historically worked in urban environments. Long Reach's strategy had to now reach the emerging black professional suburbanite. In an urban environment, people do not want strangers in their homes. Sometimes it is unsuitable to invite others into a person's home as there are safety issues to be considered. In urban churches, people must learn to be creative; people can meet elsewhere. For example, they can meet at the church or at a restaurant or at a library. Determining one person who will host all the meetings can help. This makes it less stressful for those who would not want to host the group.

Despite the fear issues, it is possible to break the barriers of having someone in their homes. For example, someone may drop off something at the door, talk for five minutes and then leave. Then he or she increases the duration of the visit. As this person gradually introduces him- or herself to the person's environment, usually the visitor will be invited inside. It is a process for people to let down their guard. Eventually people find that they can entertain the idea of hosting a meeting.

Suburban churches have different issues. In the suburbs there is a lack of community. People don't sense closeness with neighbors. They do not have to leave the house. Everything we need is on this side of the door. The church has to break down these barriers. How Long Reach does this is again through both spontaneous and planned visits. They try to find ways in which people can meet together in their neighborhoods, casually and formally.

As churches grow, they seem to fall into the trap of becoming an exclusive club. The people don't have time to develop relationships with unbelievers because of so much activity in the church. At Long Reach, they recruit unbelievers intentionally.

How do they do this? Suzanne Haley gave the following example:

Let's say we have a project we want to do with the teens. We don't have to go to the same 20 percent of our members who do 80 percent of the work. Instead, we put an ad in the local newspaper to get others outside the church to be involved. The project is sponsored by Long Reach and meetings are held there. During the meetings, we share the awesome vision of the project. These outside people sign up and we now have their phone numbers. We publish them and five people call them between the first and second meeting. Relationships are being forged. These projects are intentional evangelism; they are our only agenda; our agenda is not hidden. When a project is taking place, the outsiders are now close to some Christians. So many people get saved this way. The common cause or concern (youth project) builds a bridge in the community across the chasm between them and the church. Everyone feels justified and valuable because of what is done. Appreciation is demonstrated time and time again. Because we are a church, we pray for the event and the people. People find their lives are changing. They are connected because the project focus went to the relational level.

Ms. Haley gave us another example from Long Reach: They formed a church step team but accepted non-Christians in order to let them experience community for a step show. Teens then asked the non-Christians to their cell groups while rehearsing for the show.

Long Reach Church of God has developed a relaxed cell-church model because of the explosive growth of their community and their unique position in the region. Due to several of its outreach ministries, which include a regional Christian school, Bishop Davis and the team have become trusted community leaders. As a result of these dynamics, Long Reach has started four different types of cell groups: (1) shepherd cells, (2) ministry cells, (3) special-interest cells and (4) evangelism cells.

ENDNOTES

Chapter 1

1. The Census Bureau reports that as of March 2002 there were approximately 287 million residents in the United States, of which 36 million were black and about 198 million were non-Hispanic white (Sources: "The Black Population in the United States: 2002," by Jesse McKinnon, issued April 2003, p. 1; and "Monthly National Population Estimates," http://eire.census.gov/popest/data/national/tables/NA-EST2003-01.php). Data related to topics of conversation were drawn from OmniPoll S-03, conducted by Barna Research Group in May 2003 among a national sample of 1,002 adults (including 615 whites, 166 blacks). The discussion topics evaluated were spiritual matters, politics, morality, the content of TV and movies, money, parenting and sports. There were significant differences related to three items. In a typical week, spirituality was discussed by 55 percent of blacks, 42 percent of whites and 30 percent of Hispanics. Fifty-eight percent of blacks discussed moral matters compared to 49 percent of whites and 40 percent of Hispanics. Whites were more likely to discuss political issues and events (55 percent) than were blacks (41 percent) or Hispanics (42 percent).

2. Similar levels of relational difficulties were discovered through OmniPoll 1-02 (N=1,006, with 663 whites and 134 blacks), which showed mending or developing family relationships as the biggest need for 10 percent of blacks and 8 percent of whites; through OmniPoll 2-03 (N=1,024, including 661 whites and 140 blacks), which revealed that 60 percent of blacks and 66 percent of whites feel personally connected to others; through OmniPoll 1-01 (N=1,005, of which 623 were white and 179 black adults), which found that 60 percent of blacks and 55 percent of whites admitted that they have experienced times when their anger has had a negative effect on a relationship; and through OmniPoll 2003 Cume (N=4,045, with 2,582 whites and 611 blacks), which indicated that the percentage of blacks who had been married and then divorced was 25 percent compared to 27 percent among whites. Data collected through OmniPoll 1-01 showed that 46 percent of blacks and 44 percent of whites felt they were "too busy" and 32 percent of each group described themselves as "stressed out."

3. Two-thirds of both blacks and whites (66 percent of each segment) said they were "very happy with their life," according to OmniPoll 2003 Cume (N=4,045, with 2,582 whites and 611 blacks). The same survey revealed

that similar proportions of whites and blacks (23 percent and 28 percent, respectively) contended that "life is getting more stressful." In OmniPoll 1-02 (N=1,006, with 663 whites and 134 blacks) we learned that 22 percent of each group claimed to be "completely satisfied with your life today." Equivalent proportions of both segments described themselves as "skeptical" (55 percent of blacks, 60 percent of whites) in OmniPoll 1-00 (N=1,002, with 712 whites and 125 blacks).

4. Whites were twice as likely to be "upscale" (college educated and with an annual household income exceeding $60,000) while blacks were twice as likely to be "downscale" (no college degree and earning under $20,000). This was based on OmniPoll 2003 Cume (N=4,045, with 2,582 whites and 611 blacks). OmniPoll 1-02 (N=1,006, with 663 whites and 134 blacks) found that blacks were twice as likely to describe themselves as being "in serious debt." In OmniPoll 1-01 we learned that blacks were twice as likely to say they were "personally struggling with finances" (51 percent versus 26 percent). Blacks were nearly four times more likely than whites to state that they were attending some type of 12-step or substance-abuse recovery group (OmniPoll 1-02, N=1,006, containing 663 whites and 134 blacks). The same study revealed that blacks were 56 percent more likely to admit that they are "dealing with an addiction in their life."

5. In OmniPoll 1-02 (N=1,006, with 663 whites and 134 blacks) 17 percent of blacks and 10 percent of whites described themselves as "lonely." The differences were even more vivid in that blacks were twice as likely to say they were "trying to find a few good friends" (46 percent versus 26 percent, based on OmniPoll 1-01, N=1,005, with 623 whites and 179 blacks).

6. In a typical month, blacks are more than twice as likely as whites to engage in sexual relations with someone to whom they are not married (OmniPoll 2003 Cume, N=4,045, with 2,582 whites and 611 blacks). Black adults were nearly twice as likely to read pornographic magazines, watch porn movies or visit pornographic websites (OmniPoll S-03, N=1,002, including 615 whites and 166 blacks).

7. Sources of these statistics include *The Black Population in the United States: March 2002* (Washington, D.C: U.S. Census Bureau, April 2003), pp. 3-4; *Statistical Abstract of the United States* (Washington, D.C: U.S. Census Bureau, 2003), pp. 46-47, 51, 59-60, 63-64, 70.

8. George Barna, *African Americans and Their Faith*, national random sample of 800 black adults (Oxnard, CA: The Barna Group, 1999), p. 23.

9. Our OmniPoll 1-00 survey discovered that 48 percent of blacks felt they were "often misunderstood by other people" but just 29 percent of whites felt similarly.

10. In OmniPoll 1-01 (N=1,005) we learned that blacks were twice as likely as whites to believe that their hard work has earned them a better quality of

life than they have experienced. Further, 91 percent of blacks admitted to being totally committed to getting ahead, compared to just 63 percent of whites who shared that vision (OmniPoll S-02, N=1,007, 638 whites, 143 blacks).

11. Overall, 58 percent of blacks and only 28 percent of whites said they are "searching for meaning and purpose in life" (OmniPoll 1-01).

12. Barna, *African Americans and Their Faith*, p. 15.

13. Three-quarters of blacks alluded to their concern about the future, transcending the two-thirds of whites who shared that concern, according to the data from OmniPoll 1-01.

14. Barna, *African Americans and Their Faith*, p. 31.

15. Ibid.

16. OmniPoll 2003 Cume (N=4,045, with 2,582 white and 611 black) shows that only 3 percent of black adults possess a biblical worldview. This means that just 3 percent believe in absolute moral truth; contend that such truth is contained in the Bible; and believe in God as being the omnipotent and omniscient ruler of the universe, in Christ's having lived a sinless life, in the reality of Satan, that salvation is through grace alone, that the Bible is totally accurate in all of its teachings and that they have a personal responsibility to share their faith in Jesus with non-Christians.

17. We compared the life goals of people by interviewing 800 black adults and 1,039 white adults in 1999. While 94 percent of blacks listed having a close relationship with God, just 72 percent of whites concurred. Six out of 10 blacks prioritized influencing people's lives, compared to only 39 percent of whites.

Chapter 2

1. Our apologies to female pastors for the use of the male pronoun in referring to pastors throughout this book. Unlike many other languages, the English language creates problems related to the use of gender-exclusive pronouns. We readily acknowledge that women serve as pastors in churches and generally play a more significant leadership role in black churches than in most other churches. The use of "he" in reference to pastors is not intended to diminish the calling or significance of black female pastors but rather to reflect the fact that more than 9 out of 10 senior pastors are male and that the constant use of "he or she" is an awkward contrivance.

2. Floyd Massey, Jr., and Samuel Barry McKinney, *Church Administration in the Black Perspective* (Valley Forge, PA: Judson Press, 1976), pp. 35-36.

3. "Emmett Till," *The Heroism Project*. http://www.heroism.org/class/1950/heroes/till.htm (accessed April 12, 2004).

4. Bob Dylan, "The Death of Emmett Till," Copyright © 1963; renewed 1991 Special Rider Music.

5. Massey and McKinney, *Church Administration in the Black Perspective,* p. 18.

6. Ibid.

Chapter 3

1. *Random House Webster's College Dictionary,* s.v. "disciple."

2. Milton C. Sernett, ed., *African American Religious History: Documentary Witness* (Durham, NC: Duke University Press, 1999), p. 232.

3. These data are drawn from national telephone surveys conducted by the Barna Research Group among a representative, random sample of the population during 2003. The total sample size was 4,045 adults, which included 2,582 whites, 611 blacks and 506 Hispanics.

4. Dale P. Andrews, *Practical Theology for Black Churches* (London: Westminster John Knox Press, 2002), p. 1.

5. Ibid., pp. 5-6, attributed to James Deotis Roberts (p. 79).

6. Tom Peters, *Thriving on Chaos: Handbook for a Management Revolution* (New York: Harper and Row Publishers, 1987), p. 3.

Chapter 4

1. Judson Cornwall, *Let Us Worship* (South Plainfield, NJ: Bridge Publishing, 1983), p. 48.

2. George Barna, *The Habits of Highly Effective Churches* (Ventura, CA: Regal Books, 1999), pp. 84-85.

3. Ibid.

4. Albert J. Raboteau, *Slave Religion: The "Invisible Institution" in the Antebellum South* (New York: Oxford University Press, 1978), p. 248.

5. Robin D. G. Kelley and Earl Lewis, *A History of African Americans: To Make Our World Anew* (Oxford, UK: Oxford University Press, 2000), p. 189.

6. Thomas Higgison, quoted in Milton C. Sernett, ed., *African American Religious History: Documentary Witness* (Durham, NC: Duke University Press, 1999), p. 113.

7. James H. Cone, *Sanctification, Liberations and Black Worship,* vol. 35, no. 2 (July 1978), p. 2.

8. Robert Anderson, quoted in Albert J. Raboteau, *Slave Religion,* p. 65.

9. Daniel Payne, quoted in Albert J. Raboteau, *Slave Religion,* pp. 68-69.

10. Phyllis Wheatley, quoted in Albert J. Raboteau, *Slave Religion,* p. 335.

11. *Gospel Music Association.* http://www.gospelmusic.org (accessed January 6, 2003).

12. Barna, *The Habits of Highly Effective Churches*, p. 105.

13. Ibid., pp. 101-102.

14. George Barna, *African Americans and Their Faith*, national random sample of 800 black adults (Oxnard, CA: The Barna Group, 1999), p. 53.

15. Brenda Eatman Aghahowa, *Praising in Black and White: Unity and Diversity in Christian Worship* (Cleveland, OH: United Church Press, 1996), p. 55.

16. W. E. B. DuBois, quoted in James H. Cone, *Sanctification, Liberations and Black Worship*, p. 5.

17. Cone, *Sanctification, Liberations and Black Worship*, p. 5.

18. Hozell C. Francis, *Church Planting in the African American Context* (Grand Rapids, MI: Zondervan Publishing House, 1999), pp. 62, 64.

19. George Barna, *African Americans and Their Faith*, p. 52.

20. Overall, 70 percent of black pastors use the *King James Version*. The runners-up include the *New International Version* (8 percent), *Revised Standard Version/New Revised Standard Version* (7 percent) and *New King James Version* (6 percent).

21. Barna, *The Habits of Highly Effective Churches*, pp. 91-92.

Chapter 5

1. These figures are based upon our annual national tracking study of faith practices and beliefs. The 2004 edition, OmniPoll 1-04, was conducted in the last week of January and first week of February 2004, among 1,014 randomly sampled adults in the United States, of whom 14 percent were black.

2. C. Eric Lincoln, *Race, Religion, and the Continuing American Dilemma* (New York: Hill and Wang, 1999), p. 45.

3. Ibid.

4. Ibid.

5. C. Eric Lincoln and Lawrence H. Mamiya, *The Black Church in the African American Experience* (Durham, NC: Duke University Press, 1990), p. 50.

6. Lee N. June, *Evangelism and Discipleship in African-American Churches* (Grand Rapids, MI: Zondervan Publishing House, 1995), pp. 20-21.

7. Albert J. Raboteau, *Slave Religion: The "Invisible Institution" in the Antebellum South* (New York: Oxford University Press, 1978), p. 141.

8. June, *Evangelism and Discipleship in African-American Churches*, p. 19.

9. Data drawn from OmniPoll 1-04, conducted by the Barna Research Group in January-February 2004, among a national random sample of 1,014 adults. The study found that 49 percent of blacks said they "strongly agreed" that they have a "personal responsibility to share their religious beliefs with others who believe differently;" 33 percent of non-black adults held a similar belief.

10. George Barna, *African Americans and Their Faith*, national random sample of 800 black adults (Oxnard, CA: The Barna Group, 1999), pp. 31-32.

11. From OmniPoll 1-04, conducted by the Barna Research Group in January-February 2004, among a national random sample of 1,014 adults. The study found that 63 percent of black born-again adults and 48 percent of non-black born-again adults said they had shared their faith with a non-believer.

12. George Barna, *Evangelism That Works* (Ventura, CA: Regal Books, 1995).

13. George Barna, *The Habits of Highly Effective Churches* (Ventura, CA: Regal Books, 1999), p. 117.

14. Barna, *African Americans and Their Faith*, p. 61.

15. Tom Skinner, quoted in Lee N. June, *Evangelism and Discipleship in African-American Churches*, p. 35.

Chapter 6

1. George Barna, *African Americans and Their Faith*, national random sample of 800 black adults (Oxnard, CA: The Barna Group, 1999), p. 24.

2. Ibid., p. 23.

3. *The Boston Stategy to Prevent Youth Violence*, http://www.bostonstrategy.com/players/05_clergy/00_clergy.html (accessed December 15, 2003); Jenny Berrien and Christopher Winship, "Should We Have Faith in the Churches? Ten-Point Coalition's Effect on Boston's Youth Violence" (Boston: Harvard University, June 1999), http://www.ksg.harvard.edu/inequality/privatepapers/Winship.PDF (accessed December 15, 2003).

4. Ibid.

5. Byron R. Johnson, *The Role of African-American Churches in Reducing Crime Among Black Youth* (Philadelphia: Center for Research on Religion and Urban Civil Society, University of Pennsylvania). http://www.manhattan-institute.org/html/crrucs2001_2.htm (accessed October 23, 2002).

6. Dr. Harold Dean Trulear, "Black Churches, the Urban Youth Crisis and Youth Socialization," *Mount Pleasant Baptist Church*. www.mountpleasantbaptistchurch.com (accessed October 23, 2002).

7. Carlyle Fielding Stewart III, *African American Church Growth: Twelve Principles for Prophetic Ministry* (Nashville, TN: Abingdon Press, 1994), p. 50.

8. Dr. Andrew Billingsley, *Mighty Like a River: The Black Church and Social Reform* (New York: Oxford Press, 1999), p. 87.

9. Barna, *African Americans and Their Faith*, p. 58.

Chapter 7

1. These figures are based on interviews with 1,202 Protestant senior pastors

from a national random sample conducted during 2003. This included 902 pastors of white congregations and 156 pastors of black congregations. The data regarding household income are based on surveys among more than 4,000 adults sampled randomly from the 48 continental states during 2003. Of those adults, 2,259 were white and 484 were black.

2. E. F. Schumacher, *Small Is Beautiful: Economics As If People Mattered* (New York: Harper and Row Publishers, 1975), p. 168.

3. Arlee Griffin, Jr., *From Proclamation to Practice: A Unique African American Approach to Stewardship,* Clifford A. Jones, Sr., ed., (Valley Forge, PA: Judson Press, 1993), p. 66.

4. C. Eric Lincoln and Lawrence H. Mamiya, *The Black Church in the African American Experience* (Durham, NC: Duke University Press, 1990), p. 258.

Chapter 8

1. "Biography of Thurgood Marshall Associate Justice of the U.S. Supreme Court," *The United States Army District of Washington.* http://www.mdw. army.mil/fs-p28.htm (accessed April 30, 2004).

2. C. Eric Lincoln and Lawrence H. Mamiya, *The Black Church in the African American Experience* (Durham, NC: Duke University Press, 1990), p. 244.

3. Source unknown.

Chapter 9

1. Carlyle Fielding Stewart III, *African American Church Growth: 12 Principles for Prophetic Ministry* (Nashville, TN: Abingdon Press, 1994), p. 44.

2. Ibid.

3. Floyd Massey, Jr., and Samuel Berry McKinney, *Church Administration in the Black Perspective* (Valley Forge, PA: Judson Press, 2003), p. 22.

Appendix: Church Portraits

Family

1. George Barna, *Grow Your Church from the Outside In* (Ventura, CA: Regal Books, 2002).

2. Dr. Willie Richardson, *Reclaiming the Urban Family* (Grand Rapids, MI: Zondervan Publishing House, 1996), pp. 51-62.

Relationships

1. John P. Cotter and John K. Cotter, *What Leaders Really Do* (Boston, MA: Harvard Business School Press, 1999), p. 7.

Top Strategies for Today's Churches

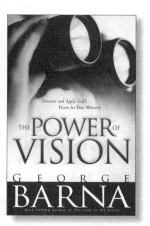

The Power of Vision
How You Can Capture and Apply God's Vision for Your Ministry
ISBN 08307.32551

To minister authentically and authoritatively, you must first clarify your vision—then embrace it and make it the heartbeat of your church. Learn how vision is a clear mental image of the best future that God imparts to His chosen servants and how you can remake your church and ministry into this ideal!

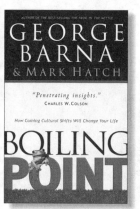

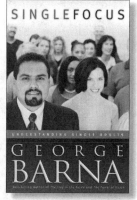

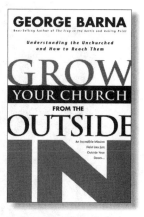

Boiling Point
How Coming Cultural Shifts Will Change Your Life
ISBN 08307.33051

Boiling Point provides contemporary statistics that illustrate the shifting beliefs and attitudes of society today. The Church is entering a time of rapid change in which it must anticipate the world's spiritual needs to meet them head-on. If you want to understand life in the third millennium, *Boiling Point* is your key.

Single Focus
Understanding Single Adults
ISBN 08307.29585

Most pastors know very little about this mushrooming population group. *Single Focus* bridges the information gap, revealing the mindsets, morals and lifestyles of singles from all age groups—and probing everything from their heartfelt hopes to their unspoken fears. If you want to understand singles, start here!

Grow Your Church from the Outside In
Understanding the Unchurched and How to Reach Them
ISBN 08307.30877

Backed by rock-solid research, here is a real-world profile of the unchurched including their values, attitudes, behaviors and beliefs. Discover these breakthrough strategies from churches that have had great success in attracting and retaining unchurched people, and then use them in your own church!

Is the Picture-Perfect Family *Truly* Achievable?

In-Laws, Outlaws and the Functional Family
A Real-World
Guide to Resolve
Family Issues
ISBN 08307.29674

Wherever you live, you want your home to be a place where God is exalted and your loved ones are protected. When it comes to the daily ungodly assaults on your family, Dr. Harry Jackson, Jr., tackles them head-on. Everything from money troubles and communication to parenting, sex, relationship problems and more!

Pastor Jackson tells it exactly like it is—and he gives you real-world answers to real-world questions. *In-Laws, Outlaws and the Functional Family* is first and foremost an action plan for safeguarding your home on all fronts. It's a book packed with wisdom and rock-solid biblical truth for life today—and every day!